Best of
NEW ENGLAND
Comforts made simple

GARDEN *of* GRAPES.

Introduction

Welcome to the delightful world of "Best of New England Comforts made simple: Simplicity Meets Tradition," a culinary journey through the heartwarming and timeless flavors of New England. In these pages, you'll embark on a culinary adventure that celebrates the simplicity and cherished traditions of this charming region through over 100 easy-to-follow recipes that are sure to warm your heart and fill your belly.

As you turn the pages of this cookbook, you may wonder what inspired its creation. The answer is a deep-rooted love for New England's culinary heritage. The author, deeply passionate about the region's rich food culture, drew inspiration from the cozy, comforting dishes that have been a part of New Englanders' lives for generations. These recipes are a celebration of the love and care that go into every meal, preserving the authentic flavors while making them accessible to home cooks like you.

Inside this cookbook, you will find a treasure trove of recipes that reflect the essence of New England. From hearty chowders to succulent seafood, from classic clam bakes to delectable desserts, each dish is crafted with an emphasis on simplicity without compromising on taste. Whether you are a seasoned chef or just starting your culinary journey, these recipes have been thoughtfully curated to ensure that anyone can recreate the magic of New England cuisine in their own kitchen.

Get ready to experience the warmth and comfort of a New England kitchen in the comfort of your own home. Explore the pages that follow, and you'll discover recipes that will transport you to the cozy shores, picturesque landscapes, and vibrant food markets of this beautiful region. So, tie on your apron, gather your ingredients, and let's embark on a culinary adventure that celebrates the timeless traditions and heartwarming simplicity of New England's culinary heritage.

Cooking Philosophy or Approach

At the heart of "Best of New England Comforts made simple: Simplicity Meets Tradition" lies the author's deeply rooted approach to cooking and food. This cookbook embodies a philosophy that cherishes the authenticity and purity of ingredients while embracing the simplicity of preparation techniques.

The author's culinary journey is guided by a profound appreciation for the flavors and traditions of New England. With a dedication to preserving the essence of this region's cuisine, each recipe is carefully crafted to ensure that the flavors shine through without unnecessary complexity. This approach celebrates the honesty of ingredients, allowing the natural tastes and textures to take center stage.

Throughout the pages of this cookbook, you'll find an emphasis on the use of fresh, locally sourced ingredients, paying homage to the rich agricultural and coastal bounty that New England offers. From the succulent seafood caught in its pristine waters to the vibrant produce harvested from its fertile soils, every dish showcases the region's culinary treasures.

In terms of cooking techniques, you'll discover a blend of time-honored methods and modern adaptations. While some recipes adhere closely to traditional preparation methods, others offer contemporary twists that make them accessible and convenient for today's home cooks. This balance ensures that both seasoned chefs and novice cooks can embark on a flavorful culinary journey.

The author's approach to food is not just about creating delicious meals; it's also about fostering a sense of connection to the culture, history, and people of New England. Each recipe is a tribute to the generations of cooks who have passed down their knowledge, and every dish is an invitation to savor the stories that make New England's culinary heritage so special.

So, as you delve into the recipes within these pages, you'll experience the author's philosophy of embracing the simplicity of New England's culinary traditions, allowing you to bring the comforting and heartwarming flavors of the region to your own table with ease and authenticity.

Yankee Pot Roast
See page, 13

Tips for Successful Cooking

In the culinary journey through "Best of New England Comforts made simple: Simplicity Meets Tradition," success in the kitchen is not just about following recipes—it's also about understanding the nuances of New England cuisine and harnessing the flavors of the region. Here are some general cooking tips and techniques that will prove invaluable as you embark on this delightful adventure:

Quality Ingredients: Start with the freshest, highest-quality ingredients you can find. Seek out local produce, seafood, and dairy whenever possible to capture the authentic flavors of New England.

Preparation Matters: Take your time to properly prep ingredients. Whether it's dicing onions for chowder or shucking corn for succotash, precise preparation ensures even cooking and better flavor distribution.

Balancing Flavors: New England cuisine often strikes a balance between sweet and savory, so be mindful of this interplay. Sweet maple syrup, for instance, can complement the savory richness of bacon in a harmonious way.

Seasoning Skill: Seasoning is key. Learn how to season your dishes with salt and pepper to enhance their natural flavors. Consider using sea salt or kosher salt for a more nuanced taste.

Chowder Creaminess: When making creamy chowders, add dairy slowly and stir constantly to prevent curdling. Warm the dairy before adding it to the chowder to help maintain a smooth texture.

Fresh Seafood: When working with seafood, especially shellfish, make sure it's fresh. Discard any open or damaged shells, as they may not be safe to consume.

Herbs and Spices: Experiment with local herbs and spices to enhance your dishes. Think about using dried thyme, bay leaves, and fresh parsley for added depth of flavor.

Baking Tips: If you're diving into the world of New England pies and desserts, preheat your oven properly, and follow the recommended baking times closely. A perfectly baked pie crust should be golden brown and flaky.

Local Flavors: Embrace regional specialties like cranberries, blueberries, and lobster. Incorporate them into your dishes to capture the essence of New England.

Taste as You Go: Throughout the cooking process, taste your dishes and adjust seasoning as needed. It's easier to add salt or other seasonings gradually than to correct an overly salty dish.

Simmering Techniques: Many New England classics benefit from slow simmering to develop rich flavors. Be patient and let soups and stews simmer on low heat to achieve their full potential.

Sharing Traditions: New England cooking often revolves around communal gatherings. Share your creations with friends and family to create cherished memories.

By keeping these tips in mind, you'll not only master the art of New England cooking but also create memorable meals that celebrate the region's culinary traditions. Enjoy your journey through this cookbook, and may each dish you prepare bring a taste of New England's warmth and tradition to your table.

Roast Turkey with Cranberry Sauce
See page, 18

Kitchen Essentials

To embark on your culinary adventure through the pages of "Best of New England Comforts made simple: Simplicity Meets Tradition," it's important to have a well-equipped kitchen. Here's a list of essential kitchen tools and equipment that you'll frequently use in the recipes, along with some tips on how to use them effectively:

Chef's Knife: Invest in a good-quality chef's knife for chopping, slicing, and dicing. Keep it sharp for precise cutting.

Cutting Board: Use a sturdy cutting board to protect your countertops. Wooden or plastic boards are easy to clean and maintain.

Pots and Pans: A variety of pots and pans in different sizes, including a stockpot, saucepans, and skillets, will be handy for soups, stews, and sautéing.

Dutch Oven: A heavy-duty Dutch oven is ideal for slow-cooking dishes like stews and braises. It distributes heat evenly and can go from stovetop to oven.

Baking Sheets: Half-sheet and quarter-sheet baking sheets are versatile for roasting vegetables, baking pies, and making biscuits.

Mixing Bowls: A set of mixing bowls in various sizes is essential for preparing and combining ingredients.

Whisk: A whisk is great for mixing batters, sauces, and dressings. Look for one with a comfortable grip.

Measuring Cups and Spoons: Accurate measurements are crucial. Use dry and liquid measuring cups and spoons for precise ingredient portions.

Food Processor or Blender: These appliances are handy for pureeing soups, making sauces, and blending smoothies.

Spatulas and Wooden Spoons: Have a variety of spatulas and wooden spoons for stirring, flipping, and scraping.

Microplane Grater: Perfect for zesting citrus fruits, grating cheese, and adding finely grated ingredients to recipes.

Oven Thermometer: Ensure your oven's accuracy for baking and roasting by using an oven thermometer.

Cooling Racks: These are essential for cooling baked goods and allowing air circulation to prevent sogginess.

Pastry Brush: Use a pastry brush for glazing pastries or brushing on marinades.

Lids and Covers: Keep lids and covers for your pots and pans handy to control cooking temperatures and prevent splatters.

Timer: Use a kitchen timer to keep track of cooking and baking times accurately.

Peeler: A vegetable peeler makes quick work of peeling potatoes, carrots, and other veggies.

Can Opener: For recipes that call for canned ingredients, a reliable can opener is a must.

Colander or Strainer: Use these to drain pasta, rinse vegetables, or strain liquids from solids.

Meat Thermometer: Ensure your meats are cooked to the desired doneness with a meat thermometer.

Remember to clean and maintain your kitchen tools and equipment regularly to prolong their lifespan and ensure safe and efficient cooking. With these essential kitchen items at your disposal and the tips on how to use them effectively, you'll be well-prepared to tackle the delicious recipes within this cookbook and create culinary delights that capture the essence of New England comfort food. Happy cooking!

Flavor Pairing Suggestions

While "Best of New England Comforts made simple: Simplicity Meets Tradition" offers a plethora of tried-and-true recipes, it's also a source of inspiration for your culinary creativity. Here are some flavor pairing suggestions and ideas for complementary ingredients that work beautifully together, allowing you to experiment and craft your own delicious New England-inspired dishes:

Maple and Bacon: The sweet richness of pure maple syrup pairs wonderfully with the smoky, salty flavor of bacon. Drizzle maple syrup over bacon-wrapped scallops or use it as a glaze for pork dishes.

Apples and Cheddar: New England is famous for its apples and artisanal cheddar cheese. Combine the two in savory pies, salads, or grilled cheese sandwiches for a delightful contrast of sweet and savory.

Corn and Lobster: Sweet corn and succulent lobster are iconic New England ingredients. Create a creamy corn and lobster chowder or a refreshing corn and lobster salad with a citrus vinaigrette.

Cranberry and Orange: The tartness of cranberries pairs harmoniously with the bright citrus flavors of oranges. Use this combination in sauces, marinades, or quick breads for a burst of vibrant flavor.

Clams and Garlic: The briny taste of clams is beautifully enhanced by the aromatic essence of garlic. Sauté garlic and clams together with white wine and fresh herbs for a classic New England clam dish.

Pumpkin and Nutmeg: Embrace the flavors of fall by combining the earthy sweetness of pumpkin with the warm spice of nutmeg. Incorporate this duo into pies, muffins, and soups.

Blueberries and Lemon: Blueberries' natural sweetness pairs exquisitely with the bright, zesty notes of lemon. Create blueberry lemon bars, pancakes, or a tangy blueberry-lemon sauce for desserts and breakfast treats.

Seafood and Dill: The mild, fresh taste of dill complements a wide range of seafood dishes. Use it as a garnish for grilled fish, in creamy seafood sauces, or in a dill-infused seafood salad.

Brown Butter and Sage: The nutty richness of brown butter marries beautifully with the earthy aroma of sage. Drizzle brown butter and sage sauce over pasta, roasted vegetables, or butternut squash dishes.

Cinnamon and Sugar: Create comforting desserts by combining the warmth of cinnamon with the sweetness of sugar. Use this combination to sprinkle on top of pies, cookies, or cinnamon sugar donuts.

Molasses and Ginger: The deep, rich flavor of molasses pairs wonderfully with the spicy kick of ginger. Incorporate this duo into gingerbread cookies, cakes, or molasses-glazed ham.

Thyme and Lemon: Fresh thyme and lemon zest offer a delightful balance of herbal and citrus notes. Use them in roasted chicken dishes, salad dressings, or as a seasoning for roasted vegetables.

These flavor pairing suggestions provide a starting point for your culinary experiments. Feel free to mix and match ingredients from this list to create your own unique New England-inspired recipes. Whether you're crafting savory dishes or sweet treats, the flavors of New England offer a wealth of possibilities for your culinary creativity. Enjoy exploring and savoring the rich tastes of the region!

Table of Contents

Chapter 1:
Classic Chowders and Soups

4 servings   320 cal   45 mins

Easy

New England Clam Chowder

A coastal classic that warms the soul—New England Clam Chowder. This chowder boasts tender clams, potatoes, and cream, reflecting the region's maritime heritage.

Ingredients:

2 cups fresh clams (chopped), 4 slices bacon (chopped), 1 onion (diced), 2 potatoes (cubed), 2 cups chicken broth, 1 cup heavy cream, 2 tbsp butter, 2 tbsp all-purpose flour, Salt and pepper to taste

Directions

1. Sauté bacon until crispy.
2. Remove bacon, sauté onion in bacon fat.
3. Add flour, make roux.
4. Stir in broth, cream.
5. Add potatoes, simmer until tender.
6. Stir in clams, cook until they open.
7. Season with salt and pepper.
8. Garnish with bacon.
9. Savor the coastal comfort.

Substitutions

Canned clams, vegetable broth

 4 servings

 280 cal

 40 mins

Fish Chowder

A maritime medley in a bowl—Fish Chowder. This chowder features a blend of white fish, potatoes, and herbs, capturing the essence of New England's coastal cuisine.

Ingredients:

1 lb white fish fillets (cod, haddock), 1 onion (diced), 2 potatoes (cubed), 2 cups fish or vegetable broth, 1 cup milk, 2 tbsp butter, 2 tbsp all-purpose flour, Fresh dill and parsley, Salt and pepper to taste

Directions

1. Sauté onion in butter until softened.
2. Add flour, make roux.
3. Gradually add broth and milk, whisk.
4. Add potatoes, simmer until tender.
5. Add fish, cook until flaky.
6. Season with salt and pepper.
7. Garnish with fresh herbs.
8. Savor the maritime flavors.

Substitutions

Any white fish, seafood broth

4 servings | 240 cal | 35 mins

Corn Chowder

A harvest of comfort in a bowl—Corn Chowder. This chowder showcases sweet corn, bacon, and potatoes, capturing the essence of New England's agrarian heritage.

Ingredients:

4 cups corn kernels (fresh or frozen), 4 slices bacon (chopped), 1 onion (diced), 2 potatoes (cubed), 3 cups chicken broth, 1 cup milk, 2 tbsp butter, 2 tbsp all-purpose flour, Fresh thyme, Salt and pepper to taste

Directions

1. Sauté bacon until crispy.
2. Remove bacon, sauté onion in bacon fat.
3. Add flour, make roux.
4. Gradually add broth and milk, whisk.
5. Add potatoes, simmer until tender.
6. Stir in corn, cooked bacon.
7. Season with salt, pepper, thyme.
8. Savor the harvest goodness.

Substitutions

Any type of bacon, vegetable broth

4 servings   380 cal   1 hour

Normal

Lobster Bisque

An indulgent symphony of flavors—Lobster Bisque. This bisque features rich lobster meat, tomatoes, and cream, a luxurious delight that pays homage to New England's coastal bounty.

Ingredients:

2 lobsters (cooked, meat removed), 1 onion (diced), 1 carrot (diced), 2 tomatoes (diced), 2 cups fish or seafood broth, 1 cup heavy cream, 2 tbsp butter, 2 tbsp all-purpose flour, Brandy or sherry (optional), Fresh tarragon, Salt and pepper to taste

Directions

1. Sauté onion and carrot in butter.
2. Add flour, make roux.
3. Gradually add broth, whisk.
4. Add tomatoes, simmer.
5. Blend mixture until smooth.
6. Return to heat, add lobster meat.
7. Stir in cream, brandy/sherry.
8. Season with tarragon, salt, pepper.
9. Savor the indulgence.

Substitutions

Lobster stock, cream sherry

4 servings   260 cal   30 mins

Rhode Island Clear Clam Chowder

A lighter take on a classic—Rhode Island Clear Clam Chowder. This chowder boasts a clear broth, tender clams, and simple flavors that showcase the essence of the region's clamming culture.

Ingredients:

2 cups fresh clams (chopped), 1 onion (diced), 2 potatoes (cubed), 2 cups clam broth, 2 cups water, Salt pork or bacon, Fresh parsley, Salt and pepper to taste

Directions

1. Sauté salt pork or bacon until crispy.
2. Remove pork, sauté onion in fat.
3. Add potatoes, clam broth, and water.
4. Simmer until potatoes are tender.
5. Add clams, cook until they open.
6. Season with salt, pepper.
7. Garnish with parsley.
8. Savor the coastal essence.

Substitutions

Canned clams, vegetable broth

4 servings | 320 cal | 50 mins

Seafood Stew

 A bountiful catch in a bowl—Seafood Stew. This stew features an assortment of seafood, tomatoes, and aromatic herbs, a flavorful representation of New England's coastal abundance.

Ingredients:

 1 lb mixed seafood (shrimp, mussels, fish), 1 onion (diced), 1 bell pepper (diced), 2 tomatoes (diced), 2 cups fish or seafood broth, 1 cup white wine, Fresh thyme and basil, Olive oil, Salt and pepper to taste

Directions

1. Sauté onion and bell pepper in olive oil.
2. Add tomatoes, cook until softened.
3. Add broth and wine, bring to a simmer.
4. Add seafood, cook until cooked through.
5. Season with salt, pepper, herbs.
6. Savor the coastal medley.

Substitutions

Any mixed seafood

4 servings | 280 cal | 1 hour

A hearty embrace of peas and ham—Split Pea Soup with Ham. This soup features split peas, ham, and vegetables, offering a comforting and satisfying dish that warms the soul.

Split Pea Soup with Ham

Ingredients:

2 cups dried split peas, 1 onion (diced), 2 carrots (diced), 2 celery stalks (diced), 1 smoked ham hock, 6 cups chicken broth, Fresh thyme, Salt and pepper to taste

Directions

1. Rinse split peas, soak for 1 hour.
2. Sauté onion, carrot, celery in olive oil.
3. Add split peas, ham hock, and broth.
4. Simmer until peas are tender.
5. Remove ham hock, shred meat.
6. Return meat to soup.
7. Season with thyme, salt, pepper.
8. Savor the hearty warmth.

Substitutions

Smoked turkey leg

4 servings | 220 cal | 40 mins

Potato Leek Soup

A silky blend of earthy flavors—Potato Leek Soup. This soup features tender leeks, potatoes, and cream, a harmonious combination that brings out the best of New England's seasonal produce.

Ingredients:

3 leeks (white and light green parts), 4 potatoes (peeled, cubed), 1 onion (diced), 4 cups vegetable broth, 1 cup heavy cream, 2 tbsp butter, Fresh chives, Salt and pepper to taste

Directions

1. Sauté leeks and onion in butter.
2. Add potatoes, sauté briefly.
3. Add broth, simmer until potatoes are tender.
4. Blend mixture until smooth.
5. Return to heat, stir in cream.
6. Season with salt, pepper.
7. Garnish with chives.
8. Savor the earthy blend.

Substitutions

Any type of cream

4 servings | 180 cal | 50 mins

Butternut Squash Soup

A taste of autumn in a bowl—Butternut Squash Soup. This soup highlights the sweetness of butternut squash, balanced with warm spices, making it a comforting reflection of New England's harvest season.

Ingredients:

1 butternut squash (peeled, cubed), 1 onion (diced), 2 carrots (diced), 4 cups vegetable broth, 1 cup coconut milk, 2 tbsp olive oil, 1 tsp ground cinnamon, Ground nutmeg, Salt and pepper to taste

Directions

1. Roast butternut squash with olive oil.
2. Sauté onion and carrots in olive oil.
3. Add roasted squash, broth, coconut milk.
4. Blend mixture until smooth.
5. Return to heat, add cinnamon and nutmeg.
6. Season with salt, pepper.
7. Savor the autumn warmth.

Substitutions

Any type of milk

4 servings   300 cal   1.5 hours

Baked Beans and Ham Soup

A heritage of comfort and flavor—Baked Beans and Ham Soup. This soup features tender beans, ham, and a medley of flavors that reflect the heartiness of New England's culinary traditions.

Ingredients:

1 cup dried navy beans (soaked), 1 onion (diced), 2 carrots (diced), 2 cups diced ham, 4 cups chicken broth, 1/4 cup molasses, 2 tbsp brown sugar, 1 tbsp Dijon mustard, Fresh thyme, Salt and pepper to taste

Directions

1. Rinse soaked beans, simmer until tender.
2. Sauté onion and carrot in olive oil.
3. Add ham, cook until browned.
4. Add broth, beans, and spices.
5. Simmer until flavors meld.
6. Stir in molasses, brown sugar, mustard.
7. Season with thyme, salt, pepper.
8. Savor the hearty legacy.

Substitutions

Any type of dried beans

Chapter 2:
Hearty Main Dishes

4 servings

380 cal

3 hours

Yankee Pot Roast

A slow-cooked symphony of flavors—Yankee Pot Roast. This roast features tender beef, root vegetables, and savory broth, capturing the essence of New England's hearty, homey meals.

Ingredients:

2 lbs beef chuck roast, 4 carrots (peeled, sliced), 3 potatoes (peeled, cubed), 1 onion (diced), 2 cups beef broth, 1 cup red wine, 2 tbsp olive oil, 2 tbsp tomato paste, Fresh rosemary and thyme, Salt and pepper to taste

Directions

1. Sear roast in olive oil until browned.
2. Sauté onion, carrots, and potatoes.
3. Add tomato paste, cook briefly.
4. Deglaze with red wine, reduce.
5. Place roast, veggies in a pot.
6. Add broth, herbs, salt, pepper.
7. Simmer, covered, for hours.
8. Savor the slow-cooked comfort.

Substitutions

Beef broth and red wine, mushroom broth

4 servings

320 cal

10 hours

Boston Baked Beans

A bean-filled ode to tradition—Boston Baked Beans. This dish showcases tender beans, molasses, and salt pork, embodying the historical flavors of New England's colonial heritage.

Ingredients:

2 cups dried navy beans (soaked), 1 onion (diced), 1/2 cup molasses, 1/4 cup brown sugar, 1/4 lb salt pork, 2 tsp Dijon mustard, 1 tsp cider vinegar, Salt and pepper to taste

Directions

1. Rinse soaked beans, simmer until partially cooked.
2. Sauté onion in olive oil.
3. Add molasses, sugar, mustard, vinegar.
4. Layer beans, onion, salt pork in pot.
5. Add water to cover.
6. Simmer, covered, for hours.
7. Remove lid, bake until beans are tender.
8. Savor the historic comfort.

Substitutions

Vegetarian baked beans

2 servings | 300 cal | 25 mins

Lobster Roll

A coastal indulgence between buns—Lobster Roll. This roll features succulent lobster meat, mayo, and herbs, a delicacy that captures the essence of New England's seaside pleasures.

Ingredients:

1 1/2 lbs lobster meat (cooked, chopped), 2 split-top hot dog buns, 1/4 cup mayonnaise, 2 tbsp butter, 1 tbsp lemon juice, Fresh chives, Salt and pepper to taste

Directions

1. Sauté buns in butter until toasted.
2. Mix lobster, mayo, lemon juice, chives.
3. Season with salt, pepper.
4. Fill buns with lobster mixture.
5. Savor the coastal delight.

Substitutions

Shrimp or crab meat

4 servings   400 cal   1.5 hours

Clam Bake

A seaside feast in a pot—Clam Bake. This bake features clams, lobster, corn, and potatoes, a festive gathering of flavors that embodies New England's coastal celebrations.

Ingredients:

2 lbs clams, 2 lobsters, 4 ears corn (husked), 8 red potatoes, 1 lb andouille sausage, 1 cup clam broth or water, Old Bay seasoning, Fresh parsley, Salt and pepper to taste

Directions

1. Steam clams in broth until they open.
2. Add lobsters, corn, potatoes, sausage.
3. Sprinkle with Old Bay seasoning.
4. Steam until lobsters are red and clams are cooked.
5. Savor the seaside feast.

Substitutions

Shrimp, mussels

6-8 servings

280 cal

2.5 hours

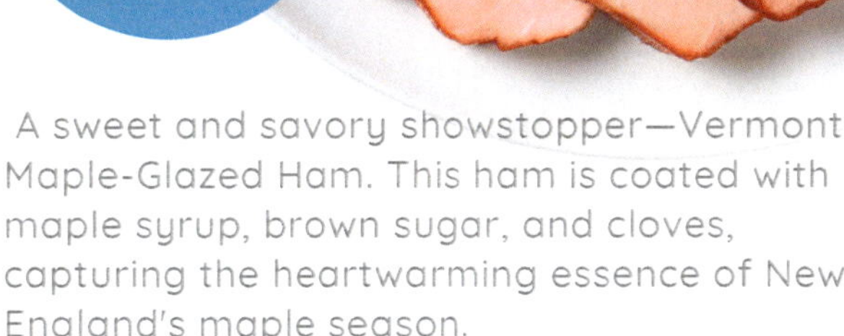

Vermont Maple-Glazed Ham

A sweet and savory showstopper—Vermont Maple-Glazed Ham. This ham is coated with maple syrup, brown sugar, and cloves, capturing the heartwarming essence of New England's maple season.

Ingredients:

5-7 lbs smoked ham (bone-in), 1 cup maple syrup, 1/2 cup brown sugar, Whole cloves, Dijon mustard, Salt and pepper to taste

Directions

1. Score ham, stud with cloves.
2. Mix maple syrup, brown sugar, mustard.
3. Brush ham with glaze.
4. Bake, brushing with glaze.
5. Savor the maple magic.

Substitutions

Honey or brown sugar glaze

8-10 servings   350 cal   3 hours

Roast Turkey with Cranberry Sauce

A festive centerpiece of flavor—Roast Turkey with Cranberry Sauce. This turkey is seasoned, roasted to perfection, and served with homemade cranberry sauce, embodying New England's Thanksgiving traditions.

Ingredients:

10-12 lbs turkey, 1 onion (quartered), 2 carrots (cut into chunks), 2 stalks celery (cut into chunks), 1 lemon (halved), Fresh rosemary and thyme, Olive oil, Salt and pepper to taste

Directions

1. Preheat oven, prepare turkey.
2. Stuff cavity with onion, lemon, herbs.
3. Rub turkey with olive oil, season.
4. Roast until cooked through.
5. Let turkey rest before carving.
6. Serve with cranberry sauce.
7. Savor the Thanksgiving feast.

Substitutions

Herbs and spices of choice

4 servings   280 cal   30 mins

Grilled Bluefish with Herb Butter

A fresh catch kissed by flames—Grilled Bluefish with Herb Butter. This bluefish is seasoned, grilled to perfection, and topped with herb butter, capturing the flavors of New England's seafood delights.

Ingredients:

4 bluefish fillets, 1/4 cup butter (softened), Fresh herbs (such as parsley, chives), 1 lemon (zested and juiced), Olive oil, Salt and pepper to taste

Directions

1. Preheat grill, season bluefish with oil, salt, and pepper.
2. Grill fish until cooked through.
3. Mix butter, herbs, lemon zest and juice.
4. Serve fish with herb butter.
5. Savor the coastal flavors.

Substitutions

Any firm fish

4 servings | 260 cal | 1 hour

Stuffed Quahogs (Stuffies)

A savory stuffing from the sea—Stuffed Quahogs (Stuffies). These clams are stuffed with a mixture of breadcrumbs, herbs, and spices, showcasing New England's love for shellfish.

Ingredients:

8-10 large quahog clams, 1 cup breadcrumbs, 1/2 cup chopped clams (reserved), 1/4 cup butter, 1 onion (diced), 1 bell pepper (diced), Fresh parsley, Ground spices (such as paprika, cayenne), Salt and pepper to taste

Directions

1. Steam quahogs until they open, remove meat, chop.
2. Sauté onion, pepper in butter.
3. Mix breadcrumbs, chopped clams, spices, herbs.
4. Combine sautéed mixture with breadcrumb mixture.
5. Stuff quahog shells with mixture.
6. Bake until stuffing is golden.
7. Savor the stuffed goodness.

Substitutions

Chopped shrimp or crab

4 servings | 240 cal | 25 mins

Baked Haddock with Ritz Cracker Topping

A crisp and tender delight—Baked Haddock with Ritz Cracker Topping. This haddock is coated with a buttery Ritz cracker topping, offering a simple and flavorful taste of New England's seafood fare.

Ingredients:

4 haddock fillets, 1 sleeve Ritz crackers (crushed), 1/4 cup butter (melted), Fresh parsley, Lemon wedges, Salt and pepper to taste

Directions

1. Preheat oven, season haddock with salt and pepper.
2. Mix crushed crackers, melted butter, parsley.
3. Spread cracker mixture over fillets.
4. Bake until topping is golden.
5. Serve with lemon wedges.
6. Savor the buttery crunch.

Substitutions

Any white fish

4-6 servings

300 cal

1.5 hours

Brown Bread and Baked Beans Casserole

A hearty embrace of flavors—Brown Bread and Baked Beans Casserole. This casserole features tender beans, molasses, and slices of brown bread, a comforting combination that harkens to New England's rustic fare.

Ingredients:

2 cans baked beans, 1 cup brown bread slices (cubed), 1/4 cup molasses, 1/4 cup brown sugar, 1/4 lb salt pork (chopped), 1 onion (diced), 1 tsp Dijon mustard, Salt and pepper to taste

Directions

1. Sauté onion and salt pork in olive oil.
2. Mix beans, brown bread, molasses, sugar, mustard.
3. Combine sautéed mixture with bean mixture.
4. Season with salt, pepper.
5. Bake until bubbly and golden.
6. Savor the rustic blend.

Substitutions

Vegetarian baked beans, vegetarian bacon

Chapter 3:
Comforting Casseroles and Pies

4 servings   400 cal   1.5 hours

Chicken Pot Pie

A flaky embrace of comfort—Chicken Pot Pie. This pie features tender chicken, vegetables, and creamy sauce, capturing the essence of cozy New England evenings.

Ingredients:

2 cups cooked chicken (shredded), 1 cup mixed vegetables (such as peas, carrots), 1/4 cup butter, 1/4 cup flour, 1 1/2 cups chicken broth, 1/2 cup milk, Fresh thyme and parsley, 1 package store-bought pie crusts, Salt and pepper to taste

Directions

1. Preheat oven, sauté vegetables in butter.
2. Add flour, cook briefly.
3. Gradually add broth, milk, stirring.
4. Simmer until thickened.
5. Stir in chicken, herbs, salt, pepper.
6. Line pie dish with crust.
7. Add filling, cover with second crust.
8. Bake until golden.
9. Savor the comforting layers.

Substitutions

Rotisserie chicken

4 servings | 380 cal | 1.5 hours

Shepherd's Pie

A savory tribute to simplicity—Shepherd's Pie. This pie features ground meat, vegetables, and mashed potatoes, a humble and hearty dish that embodies New England's comfort.

Ingredients:

1 lb ground lamb or beef, 1 onion (diced), 2 carrots (diced), 1 cup frozen peas, 1 cup beef broth, 2 cups mashed potatoes, 2 tbsp butter, Fresh thyme and rosemary, Salt and pepper to taste

Directions

1. Sauté onion, carrots until tender.
2. Add ground meat, cook until browned.
3. Add peas, broth, herbs, salt, pepper.
4. Transfer mixture to baking dish.
5. Top with mashed potatoes.
6. Dot with butter.
7. Bake until potatoes are golden.
8. Savor the rustic layers.

Substitutions

Ground turkey or chicken

4 servings **320 cal** **40 mins**

Seafood Casserole

A coastal medley in a dish—Seafood Casserole. This casserole features a harmony of seafood, creamy sauce, and breadcrumbs, a flavorful celebration of New England's maritime bounty.

Ingredients:

1 lb mixed seafood (such as shrimp, scallops, fish), 1/2 cup breadcrumbs, 1/2 cup heavy cream, 1/4 cup white wine, 1/4 cup chicken broth, 1/4 cup grated Parmesan cheese, Fresh parsley, Salt and pepper to taste

Directions

1. Preheat oven, arrange seafood in baking dish.
2. Mix breadcrumbs, Parmesan, parsley.
3. Combine cream, wine, broth, salt, pepper.
4. Pour over seafood.
5. Top with breadcrumb mixture.
6. Bake until golden and bubbly.
7. Savor the coastal blend.

Substitutions

Any seafood of choice

4 servings   340 cal   2.5 hours

New England Boiled Dinner

A traditional feast of flavors—New England Boiled Dinner. This dish features beef, cabbage, potatoes, and carrots, a wholesome meal that reflects New England's history and hearty fare.

Ingredients:

2 lbs beef brisket or corned beef, 1 head cabbage (quartered), 4 potatoes (peeled, halved), 4 carrots (peeled, halved), 1 onion (quartered), 1 tsp whole peppercorns, Fresh parsley, Salt to taste

Directions

1. Place beef in large pot, cover with water.
2. Bring to boil, skim surface.
3. Add onion, peppercorns, salt.
4. Simmer until beef is tender.
5. Add potatoes, carrots, simmer.
6. Add cabbage, simmer until tender.
7. Savor the hearty medley.

Substitutions

Smoked sausage

4 servings   350 cal   1.5 hours

Lobster Pie

A decadent delight of the sea—Lobster Pie. This pie features succulent lobster meat, buttery sauce, and flaky crust, capturing the indulgence of New England's coastal luxury.

Ingredients:

1 lb lobster meat (cooked, chopped), 1/4 cup butter, 1/4 cup flour, 1 1/2 cups milk, 1/4 cup white wine, 1 package store-bought pie crusts, Fresh chives, Salt and pepper to taste

Directions

1. Preheat oven, sauté lobster in butter.
2. Add flour, cook briefly.
3. Gradually add milk, wine, stirring.
4. Simmer until thickened.
5. Stir in lobster, herbs, salt, pepper.
6. Line pie dish with crust.
7. Add filling, cover with second crust.
8. Bake until golden.
9. Savor the coastal luxury.

Substitutions

Shrimp or crab meat

4 servings   290 cal   30 mins

Baked Scallops

A delicate treasure from the sea—Baked Scallops. These scallops are coated in breadcrumbs and herbs, baked to perfection, offering a taste of New England's seaside pleasures.

Ingredients:

1 lb scallops, 1/2 cup breadcrumbs, 1/4 cup melted butter, 1 lemon (zested and juiced), Fresh parsley, Salt and pepper to taste

Directions

1. Preheat oven, season scallops with salt and pepper.
2. Mix breadcrumbs, butter, lemon zest and juice, parsley.
3. Spread breadcrumb mixture over scallops.
4. Bake until scallops are cooked and topping is golden.
5. Savor the delicate bites.

Substitutions

Any seafood of choice

4 servings   270 cal   1.5 hours

Clam Pie

A homage to the coast—Clam Pie. This pie features tender clams, buttery crust, and savory filling, a tribute to New England's clam-rich shores.

Ingredients:

2 dozen fresh clams, 1/4 cup butter, 1/4 cup flour, 1 cup milk, 1 package store-bought pie crusts, Fresh parsley, Salt and pepper to taste

Directions

1. Steam clams until they open, remove meat, chop.
2. Preheat oven, sauté clams in butter.
3. Add flour, cook briefly.
4. Gradually add milk, stirring.
5. Simmer until thickened.
6. Stir in chopped clams, herbs, salt, pepper.
7. Line pie dish with crust.
8. Add filling, cover with second crust.
9. Bake until golden.
10. Savor the coastal tribute.

Substitutions

Canned clams

4 servings   350 cal   35 mins

Vermont Cheddar Macaroni and Cheese

A comfort classic with a twist—Vermont Cheddar Macaroni and Cheese. This dish features creamy macaroni and sharp cheddar, a celebration of New England's love for cheese and comfort.

Ingredients:

8 oz elbow macaroni, 2 cups shredded Vermont cheddar cheese, 1/4 cup butter, 1/4 cup flour, 2 cups milk, 1/2 cup breadcrumbs, Fresh thyme and parsley, Salt and pepper to taste

Substitutions

Other sharp cheeses

Directions

1. Preheat oven, cook macaroni until al dente.
2. Mix cooked macaroni with shredded cheese.
3. In a saucepan, melt butter, add flour, cook briefly.
4. Gradually add milk, stirring.
5. Simmer until thickened.
6. Stir in cheese and macaroni mixture.
7. Season with salt, pepper.
8. Transfer to baking dish, sprinkle breadcrumbs on top.
9. Bake until bubbly and golden.
10. Savor the cheesy embrace.

6-8 servings   320 cal   1.5 hours

Tourtière

A taste of French Canadian heritage—Tourtière. This pie features a spiced mixture of meats encased in flaky crust, a savory delight that reflects New England's multicultural influences.

Ingredients:

1 lb ground pork, 1/2 lb ground beef, 1 onion (diced), 1/4 cup breadcrumbs, 1/4 cup beef or vegetable broth, 1/4 cup milk, 1 tsp ground cinnamon, 1/2 tsp ground cloves, 1/4 tsp ground nutmeg, 1 package store-bought pie crusts, Salt and pepper to taste

Directions

1. Sauté onion until translucent.
2. In a bowl, mix meats, breadcrumbs, broth, milk, spices, salt, pepper.
3. Line pie dish with crust.
4. Add meat mixture, cover with second crust.
5. Bake until golden.
6. Savor the multicultural blend.

Substitutions

Ground turkey or chicken

4 servings   280 cal   50 mins

Spinach and Feta Stuffed Shells

A vegetarian delight with Mediterranean flair— Spinach and Feta Stuffed Shells. These shells are filled with a mixture of spinach, feta, and herbs, offering a flavorful departure from traditional New England fare.

Ingredients:

20 jumbo pasta shells, 2 cups spinach (cooked, chopped), 1 cup crumbled feta cheese, 1/2 cup ricotta cheese, 1 egg, 1/4 cup grated Parmesan cheese, Fresh dill and oregano, Marinara sauce, Salt and pepper to taste

Directions

1. Preheat oven, cook pasta shells until al dente.
2. In a bowl, mix cooked spinach, feta, ricotta, egg, Parmesan, herbs, salt, pepper.
3. Stuff shells with mixture.
4. Spread marinara sauce in baking dish.
5. Arrange stuffed shells in dish.
6. Bake until bubbly and golden.
7. Savor the Mediterranean twist.

Substitutions

Other greens and cheeses

Chapter 4:
Breads, Muffins, and Biscuits

1 loaf   150 cal   3.5 hours

New England Anadama Bread

A story in every slice—New England Anadama Bread. This bread features molasses and cornmeal, a staple with a heritage that reflects the region's tradition.

Ingredients:

2 cups cornmeal, 2 cups boiling water, 1/2 cup molasses, 1/4 cup butter, 4 cups bread flour, 1 packet active dry yeast, Salt to taste

Directions

1. Combine cornmeal, boiling water, molasses, butter.
2. Let mixture cool to lukewarm.
3. In a bowl, dissolve yeast in warm water.
4. Mix yeast mixture, salt, flour with cornmeal mixture.
5. Knead until smooth, rise until doubled.
6. Shape into loaf, rise again.
7. Preheat oven, bake until golden.
8. Savor the rich heritage.

Substitutions

Whole wheat flour, honey

6-8 cakes 160 cal 25 mins

Johnny Cakes

A taste of history on a griddle—Johnny Cakes. These simple cornmeal cakes offer a rustic touch of New England's past.

Ingredients:

1 cup cornmeal, 1/4 cup flour, 1 tsp baking powder, 1/2 tsp salt, 1 cup milk, 1/4 cup molasses, 1 egg, Butter for cooking

Directions

1. Preheat griddle or skillet.
2. Mix cornmeal, flour, baking powder, salt.
3. In a separate bowl, mix milk, molasses, egg.
4. Combine wet and dry ingredients.
5. Spoon batter onto hot griddle.
6. Cook until bubbles form, flip and cook until golden.
7. Savor the simple history.

Substitutions

Maple syrup, honey

12 muffins

220 cal

40 mins

Cranberry Orange Muffins

A burst of tangy and sweet—Cranberry Orange Muffins. These muffins feature juicy cranberries and zesty orange, a delightful treat that encapsulates New England's flavors.

Ingredients:

2 cups flour, 1/2 cup sugar, 2 tsp baking powder, 1/2 tsp baking soda, 1/2 tsp salt, 1 cup cranberries (fresh or frozen), Zest and juice of 1 orange, 1/2 cup milk, 1/4 cup melted butter, 1 egg

Directions

1. Preheat oven, line muffin tin.
2. Mix flour, sugar, baking powder, baking soda, salt.
3. In a separate bowl, mix cranberries, orange zest, orange juice, milk, melted butter, egg.
4. Combine wet and dry ingredients.
5. Divide batter among muffin cups.
6. Bake until golden and a toothpick comes out clean.
7. Savor the tangy sweetness.

Substitutions

Blueberries

12 rolls | 180 cal | 3 hours

Parker House Rolls

A roll with a history—Parker House Rolls. These soft and buttery rolls have been savored for generations in New England.

Ingredients:

4 cups bread flour, 1/4 cup sugar, 1 packet active dry yeast, 1/2 cup milk, 1/2 cup water, 1/4 cup butter, 1 egg, Salt to taste

Directions

1. Mix flour, sugar, yeast.
2. Heat milk, water, butter until warm.
3. Combine wet and dry ingredients.
4. Knead until smooth, rise until doubled.
5. Punch down, shape into rolls.
6. Preheat oven, brush rolls with egg wash.
7. Bake until golden.
8. Savor the tradition.

Substitutions

Honey instead of sugar

8 servings

210 cal

25 mins

Cornbread

A golden companion to any dish—Cornbread. This bread features the hearty taste of corn, a versatile staple of New England's tables.

Ingredients:

1 cup cornmeal, 1 cup flour, 1/4 cup sugar, 1 tbsp baking powder, 1/2 tsp salt, 1 cup milk, 1/4 cup melted butter, 1 egg

Directions

1. Preheat oven, grease baking dish.
2. Mix cornmeal, flour, sugar, baking powder, salt.
3. In a separate bowl, mix milk, melted butter, egg.
4. Combine wet and dry ingredients.
5. Pour batter into baking dish.
6. Bake until golden and a toothpick comes out clean.
7. Savor the corny goodness.

Substitutions

Jalapeños, cheddar cheese

12 muffins · 230 cal · 40 mins

Blueberry Muffins

A burst of summer's bounty—Blueberry Muffins. These muffins feature plump blueberries, capturing the essence of New England's vibrant seasons.

Ingredients:

2 cups flour, 1/2 cup sugar, 2 tsp baking powder, 1/2 tsp baking soda, 1/2 tsp salt, 1 cup blueberries (fresh or frozen), 1 cup buttermilk, 1/4 cup melted butter, 1 egg, 1 tsp vanilla extract

Directions

1. Preheat oven, line muffin tin.
2. Mix flour, sugar, baking powder, baking soda, salt.
3. In a separate bowl, mix blueberries, buttermilk, melted butter, egg, vanilla.
4. Combine wet and dry ingredients.
5. Divide batter among muffin cups.
6. Bake until golden and a toothpick comes out clean.
7. Savor the burst of summer.

Substitutions

Lemon zest, raspberries

1 loaf   160 cal   2.5 hours

Brown Bread in a Can

A timeless treasure—Brown Bread in a Can. This bread, steamed in a can, offers a glimpse into New England's rustic past and flavors.

Ingredients:

1 cup cornmeal, 1 cup rye flour, 1 cup whole wheat flour, 1/2 cup molasses, 1 cup buttermilk, 1 tsp baking soda, 1/2 tsp salt, Raisins or currants (optional)

Directions

1. Grease and flour a coffee can.
2. Mix flours, cornmeal, baking soda, salt.
3. In a separate bowl, mix molasses, buttermilk.
4. Combine wet and dry ingredients, add raisins if using.
5. Pour batter into can, cover with greased foil.
6. Steam for 2 hours.
7. Savor the history in each slice.

Substitutions

Nuts, dried fruit

12 biscuits   170 cal   25 mins

Flaky Biscuits

A buttery embrace of warmth—Flaky Biscuits. These biscuits feature layers of tender goodness, embodying New England's love for comfort and simplicity.

Ingredients:

2 cups flour, 1 tbsp baking powder, 1/2 tsp salt, 1/2 cup cold butter (cubed), 3/4 cup milk, 1 tbsp honey, Fresh thyme, Salted butter for brushing

Substitutions

Cheddar and chives

Directions

1. Preheat oven, line baking sheet.
2. Mix flour, baking powder, salt.
3. Cut in cold butter until mixture resembles coarse crumbs.
4. In a separate bowl, mix milk and honey.
5. Add wet ingredients to dry, mix until just combined.
6. Turn dough onto floured surface, gently knead.
7. Roll out, fold in thirds, repeat.
8. Cut biscuits, place on baking sheet.
9. Bake until golden.
10. Savor the layers of comfort.

8 scones | 250 cal | 40 mins

Maple Walnut Scones

A symphony of flavors—Maple Walnut Scones. These scones feature the nutty richness of walnuts and the sweetness of maple, a delightful combination echoing New England's harvest.

Ingredients:

2 cups flour, 1/4 cup sugar, 1 tbsp baking powder, 1/2 tsp salt, 1/2 cup cold butter (cubed), 1/2 cup chopped walnuts, 1/2 cup milk, 1/4 cup maple syrup, 1 egg, Maple glaze (optional)

Directions

1. Preheat oven, line baking sheet.
2. Mix flour, sugar, baking powder, salt.
3. Cut in cold butter until mixture resembles coarse crumbs.
4. Stir in chopped walnuts.
5. In a separate bowl, mix milk, maple syrup, egg.
6. Add wet ingredients to dry, mix until just combined.
7. Turn dough onto floured surface, gently knead.
8. Pat into circle, cut into wedges.
9. Place scones on baking sheet, brush with milk.
10. Bake until golden.
11. Drizzle with maple glaze if desired.
12. Savor the autumnal blend.

Substitutions

Pecans, brown sugar

1 loaf   160 cal   3 hours

Normal

Molasses Oat Bread

A soulful union of flavors—Molasses Oat Bread. This bread features oats and molasses, a hearty creation that embodies the warmth of New England's kitchens.

Ingredients:

1 1/2 cups rolled oats, 1/2 cup molasses, 2 tbsp butter, 1 1/2 cups boiling water, 1 packet active dry yeast, 4 cups bread flour, 1 tsp salt

Directions

1. Mix oats, molasses, butter in a bowl.
2. Pour boiling water over mixture, let cool.
3. In a bowl, dissolve yeast in warm water.
4. Mix yeast mixture, salt, flour with oat mixture.
5. Knead until smooth, rise until doubled.
6. Punch down, shape into loaf.
7. Preheat oven, bake until golden.
8. Savor the hearty embrace.

Substitutions

Raisins, honey

Chapter 5:
Fresh Seafood Delights

2 servings   220 cal   20 mins

Steamed Clams with Drawn Butter

A taste of the ocean's bounty—Steamed Clams with Drawn Butter. These clams are tender and succulent, paired with a rich drawn butter, a simple yet luxurious experience by the shore.

Ingredients:

2 dozen fresh clams, 1/2 cup white wine, 2 cloves garlic (minced), Fresh parsley, 1/2 cup melted butter, Lemon wedges

Directions

1. Rinse clams thoroughly.
2. In a large pot, heat white wine and garlic.
3. Add clams, cover and steam until they open.
4. Meanwhile, melt butter and chop parsley.
5. Serve clams with melted butter, parsley, and lemon wedges.
6. Savor the briny indulgence.

Substitutions

White wine substitute

2 servings   300 cal   30 mins

Grilled Swordfish with Lemon-Dill Sauce

A taste of the sea's delight—Grilled Swordfish with Lemon-Dill Sauce. This dish features grilled swordfish, adorned with a zesty lemon-dill sauce, capturing the essence of coastal freshness.

Ingredients:

2 swordfish steaks, Olive oil, Salt and pepper to taste, Lemon-Dill Sauce: 1/2 cup Greek yogurt, Zest and juice of 1 lemon, Fresh dill, Salt and pepper

Directions

1. Preheat grill, brush swordfish with olive oil, season with salt and pepper.
2. Grill swordfish until cooked through.
3. Meanwhile, mix Greek yogurt, lemon zest, lemon juice, chopped dill, salt, and pepper.
4. Serve swordfish with lemon-dill sauce.
5. Savor the coastal harmony.

Substitutions

Greek yogurt alternatives

1 serving   380 cal   45 mins

Baked Stuffed Lobster

A feast from the depths—Baked Stuffed Lobster. This dish features succulent lobster stuffed with a flavorful mixture, a culinary celebration of the ocean's treasures.

Ingredients:

1 lobster (1.5 to 2 lbs), 1/2 cup breadcrumbs, 1/4 cup melted butter, 2 cloves garlic (minced), Fresh parsley, Lemon wedges

Directions

1. Preheat oven.
2. Split lobster in half lengthwise.
3. Remove lobster meat, chop.
4. Mix lobster meat with breadcrumbs, melted butter, minced garlic, chopped parsley.
5. Stuff lobster shells with mixture.
6. Bake until golden and bubbly.
7. Serve with lemon wedges.
8. Savor the ocean's bounty.

Substitutions

Crab or shrimp substitute

2 servings

250 cal

20 mins

Pan-Seared Scallops with Garlic Butter

A melody of flavors from the sea—Pan-Seared Scallops with Garlic Butter. These scallops are seared to perfection, bathed in a luscious garlic butter, a harmony of taste and texture.

Ingredients:

12 large sea scallops, Olive oil, Salt and pepper to taste, Garlic Butter: 1/4 cup melted butter, 2 cloves garlic (minced), Fresh parsley, Lemon wedges

Directions

1. Preheat skillet, pat scallops dry, season with salt and pepper.
2. Add olive oil to skillet, sear scallops until golden on both sides.
3. Meanwhile, mix melted butter, minced garlic, chopped parsley.
4. Serve scallops with garlic butter and lemon wedges.
5. Savor the delicate dance.

Substitutions

White wine in garlic butter

1 pizza

280 cal

40 mins

Clam Chowder Pizza

A fusion of comfort and creativity—Clam Chowder Pizza. This pizza features creamy clam chowder as a sauce, topped with clams, potatoes, and bacon, a delightful twist on tradition.

Ingredients:

1 pizza crust (store-bought or homemade), 1 cup clam chowder, 1/2 cup chopped clams, 1/2 cup diced cooked potatoes, 1/4 cup cooked bacon (crumbled), 1 cup shredded mozzarella cheese, Fresh parsley

Directions

1. Preheat oven, roll out pizza crust.
2. Spread clam chowder on crust.
3. Sprinkle chopped clams, diced potatoes, crumbled bacon.
4. Top with shredded mozzarella cheese.
5. Bake until crust is golden and cheese is melted.
6. Garnish with fresh parsley.
7. Savor the innovative twist.

Substitutions

Clam chowder alternative

2 servings   320 cal   30 mins

Maple-Glazed Salmon

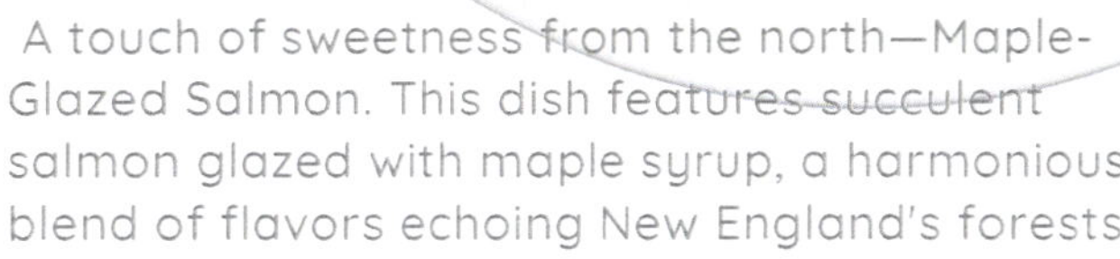

A touch of sweetness from the north—Maple-Glazed Salmon. This dish features succulent salmon glazed with maple syrup, a harmonious blend of flavors echoing New England's forests.

Ingredients:

2 salmon fillets, Olive oil, Salt and pepper to taste, Maple Glaze: 1/4 cup maple syrup, 2 tbsp Dijon mustard, 1 tbsp soy sauce, 1 clove garlic (minced), Fresh thyme

Directions

1. Preheat oven, brush salmon with olive oil, season with salt and pepper.
2. Bake salmon until almost cooked through.
3. Meanwhile, mix maple syrup, Dijon mustard, soy sauce, minced garlic, chopped thyme.
4. Brush glaze over salmon, bake until caramelized.
5. Savor the sweet and savory balance.

Substitutions

Brown sugar in glaze

2 servings 380 cal 45 mins

Lobster Newberg

A touch of elegance—Lobster Newberg. This dish features lobster in a rich, brandy-infused cream sauce, a decadent celebration of New England's coastal indulgence.

Ingredients:

2 lobsters (1.5 to 2 lbs each), 2 tbsp butter, 1 shallot (minced), 1/4 cup brandy, 1 cup heavy cream, 2 egg yolks, Salt and pepper to taste, Fresh parsley

Directions

1. Steam lobsters until cooked, remove meat and chop.
2. In a skillet, melt butter, sauté shallot.
3. Add brandy, flambé to burn off alcohol.
4. Reduce heat, add cream, simmer.
5. In a bowl, whisk egg yolks, temper with cream mixture.
6. Add lobster, cook until heated through.
7. Season with salt and pepper.
8. Serve garnished with fresh parsley.
9. Savor the refined delight.

Substitutions

Shrimp or crab

2 servings 260 cal 30 mins

Baked Stuffed Shrimp

A treasure from the sea—Baked Stuffed Shrimp. These shrimp are stuffed with a flavorful mixture and baked to perfection, a delectable delicacy that captures the essence of New England's shores.

Ingredients:

12 large shrimp (peeled and deveined), Olive oil, Salt and pepper to taste, Stuffing: 1/2 cup breadcrumbs, 1/4 cup melted butter, 2 cloves garlic (minced), Fresh parsley, Lemon wedges

Directions

1. Preheat oven, butterfly shrimp by cutting along the back, leaving the tail intact.
2. Brush shrimp with olive oil, season with salt and pepper.
3. Mix breadcrumbs, melted butter, minced garlic, chopped parsley.
4. Stuff shrimp with breadcrumb mixture.
5. Place shrimp on baking sheet, bake until shrimp are pink and opaque.
6. Serve with lemon wedges.
7. Savor the flavors of the sea.

Substitutions

Crab or scallops

2 servings   280 cal   25 mins

Grilled Striped Bass with Herbs

A melody of herbs by the shore—Grilled Striped Bass with Herbs. This dish features striped bass grilled with aromatic herbs, a taste of New England's coastal gardens.

Ingredients:

2 striped bass fillets, Olive oil, Salt and pepper to taste, Herb Mixture: Fresh herbs (such as parsley, thyme, rosemary), Lemon zest, Garlic (minced), Olive oil

Directions

1. Preheat grill, brush bass with olive oil, season with salt and pepper.
2. Mix chopped herbs, lemon zest, minced garlic, olive oil.
3. Grill bass until cooked through.
4. Sprinkle herb mixture over grilled bass.
5. Savor the coastal freshness.

Substitutions

Herbs of choice

2 servings   250 cal   25 mins

Scrod with Cracker Crumbs

A crunch of tradition—Scrod with Cracker Crumbs. This dish features tender scrod coated in buttery cracker crumbs, a classic delight that pays homage to New England's seafaring past.

Ingredients:

2 scrod fillets, Salt and pepper to taste, Cracker Crumbs: 1/2 cup crushed buttery crackers, 1/4 cup melted butter, Fresh parsley

Directions

1. Preheat oven, line baking sheet.
2. Season scrod with salt and pepper.
3. Mix crushed crackers, melted butter, chopped parsley.
4. Coat scrod fillets with cracker mixture.
5. Place scrod on baking sheet, bake until crumbs are golden.
6. Savor the maritime simplicity.

Substitutions

Lemon zest

Chapter 6:
Sides and Accompaniments

2 cups   100 cal   15 mins

Cranberry Sauce

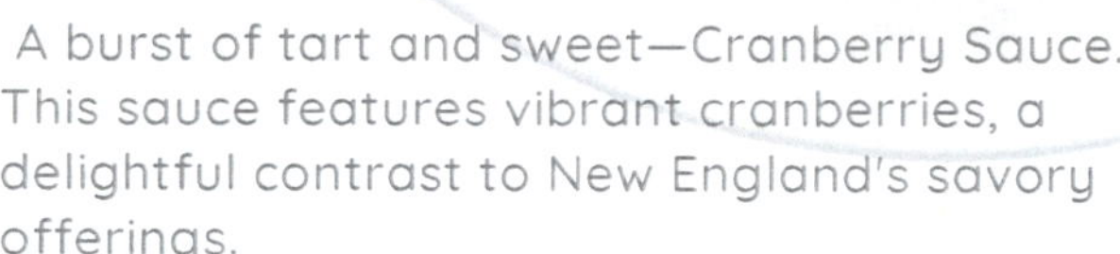

A burst of tart and sweet—Cranberry Sauce. This sauce features vibrant cranberries, a delightful contrast to New England's savory offerings.

Ingredients:

2 cups fresh cranberries, 1 cup sugar, 1 cup water, Zest and juice of 1 orange

Directions

1. Rinse cranberries, combine with sugar and water in a saucepan.
2. Bring to a boil, reduce heat, simmer until cranberries burst.
3. Stir in orange zest and juice.
4. Remove from heat, let cool.
5. Savor the tangy delight.

Substitutions

Cinnamon, nutmeg

4 servings   150 cal   20 mins

New England Coleslaw

A crisp and refreshing side—New England Coleslaw. This coleslaw features a creamy dressing, a cool and crunchy companion to hearty dishes.

Ingredients:

4 cups shredded green cabbage, 1 cup shredded carrots, 1/2 cup mayonnaise, 2 tbsp apple cider vinegar, 1 tbsp sugar, 1 tsp Dijon mustard, Salt and pepper to taste

Directions

1. In a large bowl, combine shredded cabbage and carrots.
2. In a separate bowl, whisk mayonnaise, apple cider vinegar, sugar, Dijon mustard.
3. Pour dressing over cabbage mixture, toss to coat.
4. Season with salt and pepper.
5. Refrigerate before serving.
6. Savor the crunch and creaminess.

Substitutions

Greek yogurt

4 servings **280 cal** **30 mins**

Red Flannel Hash

A symphony of colors and flavors—Red Flannel Hash. This dish features a medley of beets, potatoes, and corned beef, a hearty and rustic creation from New England's kitchens.

Ingredients:

2 cups cooked and diced corned beef, 2 cups cooked and diced potatoes, 1 cup cooked and diced beets, 1 onion (diced), 2 tbsp butter, Salt and pepper to taste

Directions

1. In a skillet, melt butter, sauté diced onion until translucent.
2. Add diced corned beef, potatoes, and beets.
3. Cook until heated through and slightly crispy.
4. Season with salt and pepper.
5. Savor the medley of flavors.

Substitutions

Fresh herbs

4 servings | 220 cal | 40 mins

Mashed Potatoes with Roasted Garlic

A creamy embrace with a touch of warmth—Mashed Potatoes with Roasted Garlic. These mashed potatoes feature the rich depth of roasted garlic, a comforting companion to New England's hearty dishes.

Ingredients:

4 large russet potatoes (peeled and diced), 1 head garlic, Olive oil, 1/2 cup milk, 2 tbsp butter, Salt and pepper to taste

Directions

1. Preheat oven, cut top off garlic head, drizzle with olive oil, wrap in foil.
2. Roast garlic until cloves are soft.
3. Boil diced potatoes until tender, drain.
4. Squeeze roasted garlic cloves into drained potatoes.
5. Add milk and butter, mash until smooth.
6. Season with salt and pepper.
7. Savor the roasted comfort.

Substitutions

Sour cream

4 servings   120 cal   25 mins

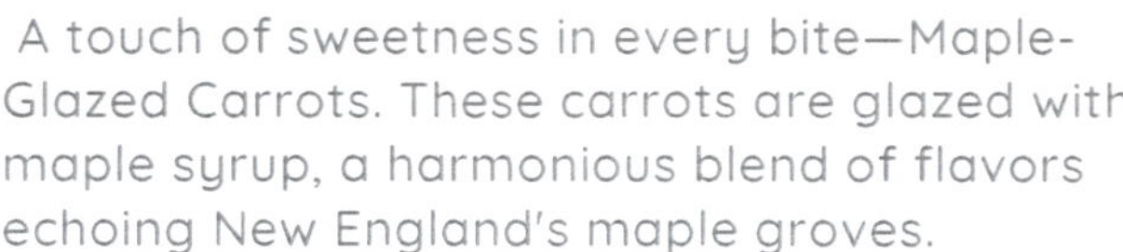

Maple-Glazed Carrots

A touch of sweetness in every bite—Maple-Glazed Carrots. These carrots are glazed with maple syrup, a harmonious blend of flavors echoing New England's maple groves.

Ingredients:

2 cups baby carrots, 2 tbsp butter, 2 tbsp maple syrup, Fresh thyme, Salt and pepper to taste

Directions

1. Steam or boil baby carrots until tender.
2. In a skillet, melt butter, add maple syrup.
3. Add steamed carrots, cook until glazed.
4. Sprinkle with fresh thyme, season with salt and pepper.
5. Savor the sweet and savory dance.

Substitutions

Brown sugar

4 servings 180 cal 35 mins

Roasted Root Vegetables

A medley of earthy delights—Roasted Root Vegetables. This dish features an array of root vegetables, roasted to perfection and offering a taste of New England's fertile soil.

Ingredients:

Assorted root vegetables (such as carrots, parsnips, turnips, beets), Olive oil, Fresh rosemary, Fresh thyme, Salt and pepper to taste

Directions

1. Preheat oven, peel and chop root vegetables into chunks.
2. Toss with olive oil, chopped rosemary, and thyme.
3. Spread vegetables on baking sheet.
4. Roast until vegetables are tender and slightly caramelized.
5. Season with salt and pepper.
6. Savor the earthy goodness.

Substitutions

Balsamic glaze

4 servings 150 cal 25 mins

Easy

Boiled Maine Potatoes

A simple and timeless pleasure—Boiled Maine Potatoes. These potatoes are boiled to perfection, a classic accompaniment to New England's hearty fare.

Ingredients:

4 Maine potatoes, Salt

Directions

1. Wash and scrub Maine potatoes.
2. Place potatoes in a pot, cover with cold water.
3. Add salt to the water.
4. Bring water to a boil, reduce heat, simmer until potatoes are tender.
5. Drain potatoes, serve as a classic side.
6. Savor the uncomplicated satisfaction.

Substitutions

Butter, fresh herbs

4 servings   160 cal   30 mins

Creamed Spinach

A velvety comfort with a touch of green—Creamed Spinach. This dish features tender spinach in a creamy sauce, a comforting companion to New England's heartier dishes.

Ingredients:

2 bunches fresh spinach (washed and trimmed), 2 tbsp butter, 2 tbsp flour, 1 cup milk, 1/4 cup grated Parmesan cheese, Nutmeg, Salt and pepper to taste

Directions

1. Blanch spinach in boiling water, drain and chop.
2. In a skillet, melt butter, add flour to make a roux.
3. Gradually whisk in milk, simmer until thickened.
4. Add chopped spinach, grated Parmesan, nutmeg, salt, and pepper.
5. Cook until spinach is heated through.
6. Savor the creamy embrace.

Substitutions

Swiss chard

4 servings | 200 cal | 40 mins

Brown Bread Stuffing

A hearty blend of tradition—Brown Bread Stuffing. This stuffing features rich brown bread, a medley of flavors that complements New England's savory offerings.

Ingredients:

4 cups cubed brown bread, 1 onion (diced), 2 celery stalks (diced), 1/4 cup butter, 2 cups chicken or vegetable broth, 2 tsp dried sage, 1 tsp dried thyme, Salt and pepper to taste

Directions

1. Preheat oven, spread cubed bread on baking sheet to toast.
2. In a skillet, sauté diced onion and celery in butter.
3. In a bowl, combine toasted bread, sautéed vegetables, dried sage, dried thyme.
4. Moisten with broth until desired consistency.
5. Season with salt and pepper.
6. Bake until golden and crispy.
7. Savor the rustic comfort.

Substitutions

Cranberries

4 servings   100 cal   15 mins

Steamed Asparagus with Lemon Butter

Easy

A burst of freshness and zest—Steamed Asparagus with Lemon Butter. This dish features tender asparagus drizzled with lemon butter, a light and vibrant side to New England's heartier meals.

Ingredients:

1 bunch asparagus (trimmed), 2 tbsp butter, Zest and juice of 1 lemon, Salt and pepper to taste

Directions

1. Steam asparagus until tender-crisp.
2. In a skillet, melt butter, add lemon zest and juice.
3. Drizzle lemon butter over steamed asparagus.
4. Season with salt and pepper.
5. Savor the balance of flavors.

Substitutions

Fresh herbs

Chapter 7:
Breakfast and Brunch Favorites

2 servings | 300 cal | 20 mins

New England Pancakes

A stack of comfort—New England Pancakes. These pancakes are light, fluffy, and simply divine, a breakfast treat that captures the essence of New England mornings.

Ingredients:

1 cup all-purpose flour, 1 tbsp sugar, 1 tsp baking powder, 1/2 tsp baking soda, 1/4 tsp salt, 1 cup buttermilk, 1 egg, 2 tbsp melted butter

Substitutions

Blueberries, chocolate chips

Directions

1. In a bowl, whisk flour, sugar, baking powder, baking soda, and salt.
2. In another bowl, whisk buttermilk, egg, and melted butter.
3. Add wet ingredients to dry, mix until just combined.
4. Heat a griddle or skillet, ladle batter onto the surface.
5. Cook until bubbles form on the surface, flip and cook until golden.
6. Serve with your favorite toppings.
7. Savor the simple joy.

2 servings   350 cal   25 mins

Blueberry Pancakes

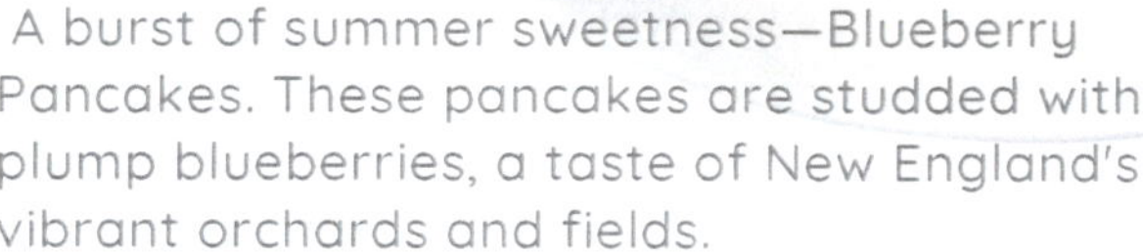

Easy

A burst of summer sweetness—Blueberry Pancakes. These pancakes are studded with plump blueberries, a taste of New England's vibrant orchards and fields.

Ingredients:

1 cup all-purpose flour, 2 tbsp sugar, 1 tsp baking powder, 1/2 tsp baking soda, 1/4 tsp salt, 1 cup buttermilk, 1 egg, 2 tbsp melted butter, Fresh blueberries

Directions

1. Whisk flour, sugar, baking powder, baking soda, and salt.
2. In another bowl, whisk buttermilk, egg, and melted butter.
3. Add wet ingredients to dry, mix until just combined.
4. Gently fold in blueberries.
5. Heat griddle or skillet, ladle batter onto the surface.
6. Cook until bubbles form, flip and cook until golden.
7. Savor the burst of flavor.

Substitutions

Fresh lemon zest

2 servings   280 cal   20 mins

Rhode Island Johnny Cakes

A taste of tradition—Rhode Island Johnny Cakes. These cornmeal pancakes are a rustic delight, a reflection of New England's heritage and love for simple pleasures.

Ingredients:

1 cup cornmeal, 1 tbsp sugar, 1/2 tsp salt, 1 cup boiling water, 1/4 cup milk, 2 tbsp melted butter

Directions

1. Mix cornmeal, sugar, and salt in a bowl.
2. Add boiling water, stir to make a thick batter.
3. Stir in milk and melted butter.
4. Heat griddle or skillet, ladle batter onto the surface.
5. Cook until crispy on both sides.
6. Savor the rustic charm.

Substitutions

Maple syrup

2 servings   320 cal   25 mins

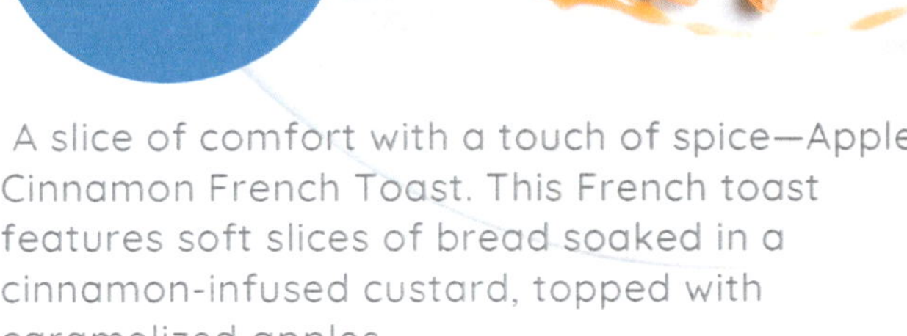

Easy

Apple Cinnamon French Toast

A slice of comfort with a touch of spice—Apple Cinnamon French Toast. This French toast features soft slices of bread soaked in a cinnamon-infused custard, topped with caramelized apples.

Ingredients:

4 slices bread, 2 eggs, 1/2 cup milk, 1/2 tsp vanilla extract, 1/2 tsp ground cinnamon, 1/4 tsp nutmeg, 1 apple (sliced), 2 tbsp butter, Maple syrup

Directions

1. In a bowl, whisk eggs, milk, vanilla, cinnamon, and nutmeg.
2. Soak bread slices in egg mixture.
3. In a skillet, melt butter, add apple slices, cook until caramelized.
4. Cook soaked bread slices until golden on both sides.
5. Serve French toast topped with caramelized apples.
6. Drizzle with maple syrup.
7. Savor the cozy indulgence.

Substitutions

Pears, raisins

2 servings | 380 cal | 30 mins

Easy

Breakfast Hash with Corned Beef

A hearty start to the day—Breakfast Hash with Corned Beef. This hash features a medley of potatoes, onions, peppers, and tender corned beef, a robust breakfast that fuels your adventures.

Ingredients:

2 cups diced cooked corned beef, 2 cups diced potatoes, 1 onion (diced), 1 bell pepper (diced), 2 tbsp butter, Salt and pepper to taste

Directions

1. In a skillet, melt butter, sauté diced onion and bell pepper.
2. Add diced potatoes, cook until crispy.
3. Add diced corned beef, cook until heated through.
4. Season with salt and pepper.
5. Savor the hearty goodness.

Substitutions

Jalapeños, cheese

2 servings

300 cal

25 mins

Lobster Omelette

A taste of luxury—Lobster Omelette. This omelette features tender lobster meat folded into fluffy eggs, a lavish indulgence that embodies New England's coastal elegance.

Ingredients:

4 large eggs, 1/4 cup cooked lobster meat, 2 tbsp butter, Salt and pepper to taste

Directions

1. Whisk eggs, season with salt and pepper.
2. In a skillet, melt butter over medium heat.
3. Pour eggs into skillet, cook until edges set.
4. Add lobster meat to one side of the omelette.
5. Fold omelette in half, cook until eggs are fully set.
6. Savor the oceanic opulence.

Substitutions

Fresh herbs

2 servings   350 cal   40 mins

Clam and Bacon Breakfast Pie

A savory start to the day—Clam and Bacon Breakfast Pie. This pie features a filling of tender clams and crispy bacon, a delightful combination of flavors that captures the essence of New England's shores.

Ingredients:

1 pie crust (pre-made or homemade), 1 cup chopped clams, 4 slices cooked bacon (crumbled), 1/2 cup shredded cheese, 3 large eggs, 1/2 cup milk, Salt and pepper to taste

Directions

1. Preheat oven, line pie crust with chopped clams and crumbled bacon.
2. Sprinkle shredded cheese over the filling.
3. In a bowl, whisk eggs, milk, salt, and pepper.
4. Pour egg mixture over the filling.
5. Bake until pie is set and golden.
6. Savor the savory comfort.

Substitutions

Spinach, mushrooms

1 loaf 220 cal 1 hr

Cranberry Nut Bread

A slice of autumnal bliss—Cranberry Nut Bread. This bread features tart cranberries and crunchy nuts, a warm and inviting treat that mirrors New England's changing seasons.

Ingredients:

2 cups all-purpose flour, 1 cup sugar, 1 1/2 tsp baking powder, 1/2 tsp baking soda, 1/2 tsp salt, 3/4 cup orange juice, 1 tbsp orange zest, 1 egg, 2 tbsp melted butter, 1 cup chopped cranberries, 1/2 cup chopped nuts (such as walnuts or pecans)

Directions

1. Preheat oven, grease and flour loaf pan.
2. In a bowl, whisk flour, sugar, baking powder, baking soda, and salt.
3. In another bowl, mix orange juice, orange zest, egg, and melted butter.
4. Combine wet and dry ingredients, fold in chopped cranberries and nuts.
5. Pour batter into loaf pan, bake until golden and a toothpick comes out clean.
6. Savor the seasonal delight.

Substitutions

Dried cherries

4 servings   **280 cal**   **25 mins**

Vermont Maple Breakfast Sausages

A touch of sweetness and spice—Vermont Maple Breakfast Sausages. These sausages are flavored with maple syrup and spices, a flavorful way to start the day the Vermont way.

Ingredients:

1 lb ground pork, 2 tbsp maple syrup, 1 tsp ground sage, 1/2 tsp ground thyme, 1/2 tsp ground nutmeg, 1/4 tsp cayenne pepper, Salt and pepper to taste

Directions

1. In a bowl, mix ground pork, maple syrup, sage, thyme, nutmeg, cayenne, salt, and pepper.
2. Shape mixture into patties.
3. Heat a skillet over medium heat, cook sausages until browned and cooked through.
4. Savor the sweet and savory combination.

Substitutions

Brown sugar

2 servings   300 cal   15 mins

Homemade Granola with Yogurt and Berries

A wholesome start to the day—Homemade Granola with Yogurt and Berries. This granola features oats, nuts, and dried fruits, a nourishing blend that pairs perfectly with creamy yogurt and fresh berries.

Ingredients:

2 cups rolled oats, 1/2 cup chopped nuts (such as almonds or pecans), 1/4 cup honey, 1/4 cup melted coconut oil, 1/2 tsp vanilla extract, 1/2 tsp ground cinnamon, 1/2 cup dried fruits (such as raisins or cranberries), Greek yogurt, Fresh berries

Directions

1. Preheat oven, mix oats and chopped nuts in a bowl.
2. In another bowl, whisk honey, melted coconut oil, vanilla, and cinnamon.
3. Combine wet and dry ingredients, spread mixture on baking sheet.
4. Bake until golden and crisp, stirring occasionally.
5. Let granola cool, mix in dried fruits.
6. Serve granola with Greek yogurt and fresh berries.
7. Savor the wholesome goodness.

Substitutions

Maple syrup

Chapter 8:
Comforting Desserts

6 servings   300 cal   45 mins

Apple Crisp

Warm and delightful—Apple Crisp. This dessert features tender baked apples under a crispy oat topping, a true taste of comfort on a cool New England evening.

Ingredients:

6 cups sliced apples, 1 tbsp lemon juice, 1/2 cup brown sugar, 1/2 tsp ground cinnamon, 1/4 tsp ground nutmeg, 1/2 cup all-purpose flour, 1/2 cup rolled oats, 1/4 cup cold butter (cubed), Vanilla ice cream

Substitutions

Pears, peaches

Directions

1. Preheat oven, toss sliced apples with lemon juice.
2. In a bowl, mix brown sugar, cinnamon, and nutmeg.
3. Sprinkle sugar mixture over apples, toss to coat.
4. In another bowl, combine flour and rolled oats.
5. Cut in cold butter until mixture resembles coarse crumbs.
6. Spread topping over apples.
7. Bake until apples are tender and topping is golden.
8. Serve warm with a scoop of vanilla ice cream.
9. Savor the warmth and sweetness.

6 servings   250 cal   2 hrs 30 mins

Indian Pudding

A taste of history—Indian Pudding. This dessert is a blend of cornmeal, molasses, and spices, a nostalgic treat that harks back to New England's colonial roots.

Ingredients:

1/2 cup cornmeal, 4 cups milk, 1/2 cup molasses, 1/4 cup brown sugar, 1 tsp ground cinnamon, 1/4 tsp ground ginger, 1/4 tsp ground nutmeg, 1/4 tsp salt, 2 tbsp butter, Vanilla ice cream

Directions

1. Preheat oven, grease baking dish.
2. In a saucepan, bring milk to a simmer.
3. Gradually whisk in cornmeal, cook until thickened.
4. Stir in molasses, brown sugar, spices, and salt.
5. Cook mixture until it bubbles and thickens.
6. Remove from heat, stir in butter.
7. Pour mixture into baking dish.
8. Bake until pudding is set and golden on top.
9. Serve warm with a scoop of vanilla ice cream.
10. Savor the taste of tradition.

Substitutions

Whipped cream

12 servings | 280 cal | 1 hr 30 mins

Whoopie Pies

A sweet sandwich—Whoopie Pies. These are two soft cake-like cookies filled with a creamy filling, a beloved treat that brings smiles to gatherings in New England.

Ingredients:

For cookies: 2 cups all-purpose flour, 1/2 cup cocoa powder, 1 tsp baking soda, 1/4 tsp salt, 1/2 cup unsalted butter (softened), 1 cup brown sugar, 1 large egg, 1 tsp vanilla extract, 1 cup buttermilk
For filling: 1/2 cup unsalted butter (softened), 1 cup powdered sugar, 1 cup marshmallow fluff, 1 tsp vanilla extract

Substitutions

Raspberry jam

Directions

For cookies:
1. Preheat oven, line baking sheets.
2. Whisk flour, cocoa powder, baking soda, and salt.
3. In another bowl, beat butter and brown sugar until creamy.
4. Beat in egg and vanilla.
5. Add dry ingredients and buttermilk in alternating batches.
6. Drop spoonfuls of batter onto baking sheets.
7. Bake until cookies spring back when touched.
For filling:
1. Beat butter until creamy.
2. Gradually beat in powdered sugar.
3. Beat in marshmallow fluff and vanilla.
4. Spread filling between two cookies.
5. Savor the sweet delight.

8 servings   320 cal   50 mins

Blueberry Cobbler

A burst of summer—Blueberry Cobbler. This dessert showcases plump blueberries under a golden biscuit topping, a celebration of New England's bountiful berry season.

Ingredients:

For filling: 4 cups fresh blueberries, 1/2 cup sugar, 1 tbsp cornstarch, 1 tbsp lemon juice

For topping: 1 cup all-purpose flour, 1/4 cup sugar, 1 tsp baking powder, 1/4 tsp salt, 1/4 cup cold butter (cubed), 1/4 cup milk

Substitutions

Vanilla ice cream

Directions

For filling:
1. Preheat oven, mix blueberries, sugar, cornstarch, and lemon juice.
2. Spread mixture in baking dish.
For topping:
1. Mix flour, sugar, baking powder, and salt.
2. Cut in cold butter until mixture resembles coarse crumbs.
3. Add milk, stir until dough forms.
4. Drop spoonfuls of dough over blueberry filling.
5. Bake until topping is golden and blueberries are bubbly.
6. Savor the burst of berry goodness.

6 servings | 280 cal | 1 hr 30 mins

Maple Walnut Ice Cream

A taste of the trees—Maple Walnut Ice Cream. This ice cream features the rich flavor of pure maple syrup and crunchy walnuts, a chilly treat that captures the essence of New England's sugarhouses.

Ingredients:

2 cups heavy cream, 1 cup whole milk, 3/4 cup pure maple syrup, 1 tsp vanilla extract, 1/2 cup chopped walnuts

Directions

1. In a bowl, whisk cream, milk, maple syrup, and vanilla.
2. Chill mixture in the refrigerator.
3. Pour mixture into ice cream maker, churn according to manufacturer's instructions.
4. During the last few minutes of churning, add chopped walnuts.
5. Transfer ice cream to a container, freeze until firm.
6. Scoop and savor the maple magic.

Substitutions

Pecans, almonds

8 servings | 350 cal | 1 hr 30 mins

A classic delight—Boston Cream Pie. This dessert is a cake filled with creamy custard and topped with a glossy chocolate glaze, a treat that embodies the elegance of New England's capital.

Boston Cream Pie

Ingredients:

For cake: 1 1/4 cups all-purpose flour, 1 1/4 tsp baking powder, 1/4 tsp salt, 1/2 cup unsalted butter (softened), 1 cup sugar, 3 large eggs, 1/2 cup milk, 1 tsp vanilla extract

For custard filling: 2 cups milk, 4 large egg yolks, 1/2 cup sugar, 1/4 cup cornstarch, 1/4 tsp salt, 1 tsp vanilla extract

For chocolate glaze: 1/4 cup heavy cream, 2 oz semisweet chocolate (chopped)

Substitutions

Whipped cream

Directions

For cake:
1. Preheat oven, grease and flour cake pans.
2. Whisk flour, baking powder, and salt.
3. Beat butter and sugar until creamy.
4. Beat in eggs, one at a time.
5. Add dry ingredients and milk in alternating batches.
6. Pour batter into pans, bake until golden.
For custard filling:
1. In a saucepan, bring milk to a simmer.
2. In a bowl, whisk egg yolks, sugar, cornstarch, and salt.
3. Gradually whisk in hot milk.
4. Return mixture to saucepan, cook until thickened.
5. Remove from heat, stir in vanilla.
6. Chill custard.
For chocolate glaze:
1. In a saucepan, heat cream until steaming.
2. Remove from heat, add chopped chocolate, let melt.
3. Stir until smooth.
To assemble:
1. Place one cake layer on a serving plate.
2. Spread custard over cake layer.
3. Top with second cake layer.
4. Pour chocolate glaze over the top, letting it drip down the sides.
5. Savor the creamy and chocolaty elegance.

8 servings | 290 cal | 1 hr 15 mins

Raspberry Peach Pie

A taste of summer's bounty—Raspberry Peach Pie. This pie features a medley of ripe raspberries and juicy peaches, a slice of New England's orchards and berry patches.

Ingredients:

For filling: 3 cups fresh raspberries, 3 cups sliced peaches, 3/4 cup sugar, 1/4 cup cornstarch, 1/4 tsp almond extract

For crust: 2 1/2 cups all-purpose flour, 1 tsp salt, 1 cup unsalted butter (cold, cubed), 1/4 to 1/2 cup ice water

Substitutions

Vanilla ice cream

Directions

For filling:
1. Mix raspberries, peaches, sugar, cornstarch, and almond extract.
2. Let mixture sit while making the crust.
For crust:
1. Mix flour and salt.
2. Cut in cold butter until mixture resembles coarse crumbs.
3. Add ice water, a tablespoon at a time, until dough forms.
4. Divide dough in half, shape into disks, chill.
To assemble:
1. Preheat oven, roll out one dough disk, fit into pie dish.
2. Pour filling into pie crust.
3. Roll out second dough disk, place over filling.
4. Trim excess dough, crimp edges.
5. Cut slits in top crust to vent.
6. Bake until crust is golden and filling is bubbly.
7. Savor the fruity harmony.

8 servings

330 cal

1 hr 15 mins

Bread Pudding with Vanilla Sauce

A comforting classic—Bread Pudding with Vanilla Sauce. This dessert transforms stale bread into a luscious treat, served with a drizzle of creamy vanilla sauce—a taste of simple indulgence in New England.

Ingredients:

For pudding: 6 cups stale bread cubes, 2 cups milk, 3/4 cup sugar, 3 large eggs, 1 tsp vanilla extract, 1/2 tsp ground cinnamon, 1/4 tsp ground nutmeg, 1/2 cup raisins (optional)

For vanilla sauce: 1 cup milk, 1/2 cup heavy cream, 1/2 cup sugar, 3 large egg yolks, 2 tsp cornstarch, 1 tsp vanilla extract

Substitutions

Nutmeg

Directions

For pudding:
1. Preheat oven, grease baking dish.
2. Spread bread cubes in dish.
3. In a bowl, whisk milk, sugar, eggs, vanilla, cinnamon, and nutmeg.
4. Pour mixture over bread cubes.
5. Let mixture sit, press down to ensure bread is soaked.
6. Sprinkle raisins over the top.
7. Bake until pudding is set and golden.
For vanilla sauce:
1. In a saucepan, bring milk and cream to a simmer.
2. In a bowl, whisk sugar, egg yolks, and cornstarch.
3. Gradually whisk in hot milk mixture.
4. Return mixture to saucepan, cook until thickened.
5. Remove from heat, stir in vanilla.
6. Serve pudding with a drizzle of warm vanilla sauce.
7. Savor the sweet and creamy comfort.

8 servings | 260 cal | 2 hrs

Pumpkin Pie with Whipped Cream

A slice of autumn—Pumpkin Pie with Whipped Cream. This pie is a celebration of the season's signature flavor, the warm and spiced pumpkin filling topped with a dollop of velvety whipped cream.

Ingredients:

For crust: 1 1/4 cups all-purpose flour, 1/2 tsp salt, 1/2 cup unsalted butter (cold, cubed), 3 to 4 tbsp ice water

For filling: 1 3/4 cups pumpkin puree, 1 cup heavy cream, 3/4 cup packed brown sugar, 3 large eggs, 1 tsp vanilla extract, 1/2 tsp ground cinnamon, 1/4 tsp ground ginger, 1/4 tsp ground nutmeg, 1/4 tsp salt

For whipped cream: 1 cup heavy cream, 2 tbsp powdered sugar, 1 tsp vanilla extract

Substitutions

Pumpkin pie spice

Directions

For crust:
1. Mix flour and salt.
2. Cut in cold butter until mixture resembles coarse crumbs.
3. Add ice water, a tablespoon at a time, until dough forms.
4. Shape dough into a disk, chill.
For filling:
1. Preheat oven, roll out dough, fit into pie dish.
2. In a bowl, whisk pumpkin puree, heavy cream, brown sugar, eggs, vanilla, spices, and salt.
3. Pour mixture into pie crust.
4. Bake until filling is set.
For whipped cream:
1. In a bowl, beat heavy cream until soft peaks form.
2. Beat in powdered sugar and vanilla.
3. Serve pie with a dollop of whipped cream.
4. Savor the autumnal delight.

8 servings

310 cal

1 hr 15 mins

Cranberry Upside-Down Cake

A tangy twist—Cranberry Upside-Down Cake. This cake showcases vibrant cranberries caramelized with brown sugar, a perfect balance of tart and sweet, a delightful finish to a New England feast.

Ingredients:

For topping: 1/4 cup unsalted butter, 1/2 cup packed brown sugar, 2 cups fresh cranberries
For cake: 1 1/2 cups all-purpose flour, 1 1/2 tsp baking powder, 1/4 tsp salt, 1/2 cup unsalted butter (softened), 1 cup granulated sugar, 2 large eggs, 1 tsp vanilla extract, 1/2 cup milk

Substitutions

Whipped cream

Directions

For topping:
1. Preheat oven, melt butter in a saucepan.
2. Stir in brown sugar, cook until mixture is smooth.
3. Pour mixture into greased cake pan.
4. Sprinkle cranberries over the top.
For cake:
1. Mix flour, baking powder, and salt.
2. Beat butter and granulated sugar until creamy.
3. Beat in eggs, one at a time.
4. Beat in vanilla.
5. Add dry ingredients and milk in alternating batches.
6. Pour batter over cranberries in cake pan.
7. Bake until cake is golden and a toothpick comes out clean.
8. Invert cake onto a serving plate.
9. Savor the tart and sweet harmony.

Chapter 9:
Classic Drinks and Beverages

4 servings   120 cal   20 mins

Hot Mulled Cider

A warm embrace—Hot Mulled Cider. This aromatic concoction blends apple cider with spices, creating a comforting drink that warms both body and soul.

Ingredients:

4 cups apple cider, 2 cinnamon sticks, 4 cloves, 1 orange (sliced), 1/4 cup honey

Directions

1. In a pot, combine apple cider, cinnamon sticks, cloves, and orange slices.
2. Bring mixture to a simmer over low heat.
3. Let flavors meld for 15 minutes.
4. Stir in honey until dissolved.
5. Serve hot and enjoy the comforting warmth.

Substitutions

Star anise, allspice berries

1 serving   50 cal   5 mins

Clamato (Clam Juice and Tomato Juice)

A unique fusion—Clamato. This drink marries briny clam juice with tangy tomato juice, a distinctive and refreshing beverage that's beloved in coastal communities.

Ingredients:

1 cup clam juice, 1 cup tomato juice, 1/2 tsp Worcestershire sauce, 1/2 tsp hot sauce, pinch of salt and pepper

Directions

1. In a glass, combine clam juice and tomato juice.
2. Add Worcestershire sauce, hot sauce, salt, and pepper.
3. Stir well to combine.
4. Serve over ice and relish the coastal flair.

Substitutions

Celery salt, lemon wedge

8 servings   150 cal   10 mins

New England Punch

A festive delight—New England Punch. This vibrant punch features fruit juices and sparkling soda, a crowd-pleaser that adds a burst of color to gatherings and celebrations.

Ingredients:

3 cups cranberry juice, 2 cups orange juice, 1 cup pineapple juice, 1/4 cup lemon juice, 2 cups ginger ale or lemon-lime soda, orange slices for garnish

Directions

1. In a punch bowl, combine cranberry juice, orange juice, pineapple juice, and lemon juice.
2. Just before serving, add ginger ale or soda.
3. Stir gently to combine.
4. Garnish with orange slices.
5. Toast to the joyful flavors.

Substitutions

Fresh mint leaves

2 servings   60 cal   5 mins

Cranberry Spritzer

A sparkling gem—Cranberry Spritzer. This effervescent drink marries tangy cranberry juice with bubbly soda water, a zesty refresher that's both delightful and invigorating.

Ingredients:

1 cup cranberry juice, 1 cup soda water, 1/4 cup lime juice, 2 tbsp simple syrup, ice cubes

Directions

1. In a glass, combine cranberry juice and soda water.
2. Add lime juice and simple syrup.
3. Stir well to blend flavors.
4. Fill the glass with ice cubes.
5. Sip and enjoy the fizzy tang.

Substitutions

Fresh cranberries

1 serving

100 cal

5 mins

Moxie (Classic New England Soda)

An acquired taste—Moxie. This distinctive soda has a loyal following in New England, offering a unique blend of bold flavors that sparks curiosity and nostalgia.

Ingredients:

1 can Moxie soda

Directions

1. Open the can of Moxie soda.
2. Pour into a glass over ice.
3. Savor the intriguing and unique flavor.

Substitutions

None

2 servings | 180 cal | 10 mins

Maple Cream Coffee

A sweet embrace—Maple Cream Coffee. This comforting blend features the richness of coffee complemented by the sweetness of maple syrup and the creaminess of whipped cream.

Ingredients:

2 cups freshly brewed coffee, 2 tbsp maple syrup, 1/2 cup heavy cream, 1 tbsp powdered sugar

Directions

1. Brew coffee using your preferred method.
2. Stir in maple syrup while coffee is still hot.
3. In a bowl, whip heavy cream and powdered sugar until soft peaks form.
4. Pour coffee into cups, top with a dollop of whipped cream.
5. Drizzle with extra maple syrup if desired.
6. Sip and relish the cozy combination.

Substitutions

Cinnamon

1 serving   70 cal   5 mins

Cranberry Juice Cocktail

A vibrant refresher—Cranberry Juice Cocktail. This tangy and sweet drink showcases the natural beauty and flavors of cranberries, offering a burst of brightness in every sip.

Ingredients:

1 cup cranberry juice, 1/4 cup orange juice, 1/4 cup pineapple juice, 1 tsp lime juice, 1 tbsp simple syrup, ice cubes

Directions

1. In a glass, combine cranberry juice, orange juice, pineapple juice, and lime juice.
2. Add simple syrup and stir well.
3. Fill the glass with ice cubes.
4. Sip and enjoy the vibrant flavors.

Substitutions

Fresh mint sprig

1 serving   80 cal   5 mins

Clamato Michelada

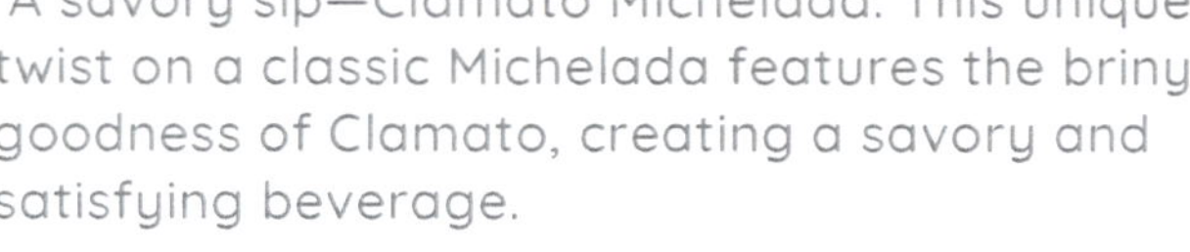

A savory sip—Clamato Michelada. This unique twist on a classic Michelada features the briny goodness of Clamato, creating a savory and satisfying beverage.

Ingredients:

1 cup Clamato juice, 1/2 cup light beer, 1/4 cup tomato juice, 1 tbsp lime juice, 1 tsp hot sauce, pinch of salt and pepper, ice cubes

Directions

1. In a glass, combine Clamato juice, light beer, tomato juice, lime juice, and hot sauce.
2. Add a pinch of salt and pepper.
3. Stir well to blend flavors.
4. Fill the glass with ice cubes.
5. Sip and relish the savory blend.

Substitutions

Celery salt, cucumber slice

2 servings · 320 cal · 10 mins

Apple Cider Doughnut Milkshake

A whimsical treat—Apple Cider Doughnut Milkshake. This playful creation blends the flavors of apple cider and doughnuts into a creamy, indulgent milkshake that captures the essence of fall.

Ingredients:

2 cups vanilla ice cream, 1 cup apple cider, 2 apple cider doughnuts, whipped cream for topping

Directions

1. In a blender, combine vanilla ice cream and apple cider.
2. Add apple cider doughnuts, broken into pieces.
3. Blend until smooth and creamy.
4. Pour into glasses and top with whipped cream.
5. Sip and delight in the whimsy of fall flavors.

Substitutions

Cinnamon sugar

4 servings   **100 cal**   **15 mins**

Blueberry Lemonade

A burst of sunshine—Blueberry Lemonade. This delightful lemonade infuses the zing of lemons with the sweetness of blueberries, creating a refreshing drink that embodies the spirit of summer.

Ingredients:

1 cup blueberries, 1/2 cup sugar, 1/2 cup water, 1/2 cup lemon juice, 3 cups cold water, lemon slices for garnish

Directions

1. In a saucepan, combine blueberries, sugar, and 1/2 cup water.
2. Simmer over medium heat until blueberries burst and sugar dissolves.
3. Strain mixture and let blueberry syrup cool.
4. In a pitcher, combine blueberry syrup, lemon juice, and cold water.
5. Stir well to combine.
6. Serve over ice, garnished with lemon slices.
7. Sip and savor the fruity fusion.

Substitutions

Mint leaves

Chapter 10:
Seasonal Specialties

 4 servings

 280 cal

 40 mins

Lobster Stew

An oceanic delight—Lobster Stew. This creamy and rich stew showcases succulent lobster meat in a velvety base, a celebration of the sea's bounty, perfect for chilly evenings.

Ingredients:

2 lobsters (cooked and meat removed), 3 cups milk, 1/4 cup unsalted butter, 1/4 cup all-purpose flour, 1/2 cup heavy cream, salt and pepper to taste, minced chives for garnish

Directions

1. In a pot, melt butter over medium heat.
2. Whisk in flour to create a roux.
3. Slowly add milk while whisking, ensuring no lumps form.
4. Bring mixture to a gentle simmer, stirring frequently.
5. Add lobster meat and heavy cream, stirring gently.
6. Season with salt and pepper.
7. Serve hot, garnished with minced chives.
8. Savor the luxurious flavors of the sea.

Substitutions

Thyme, white wine

8 servings   240 cal   1 hr 15 mins

Rhubarb Pie

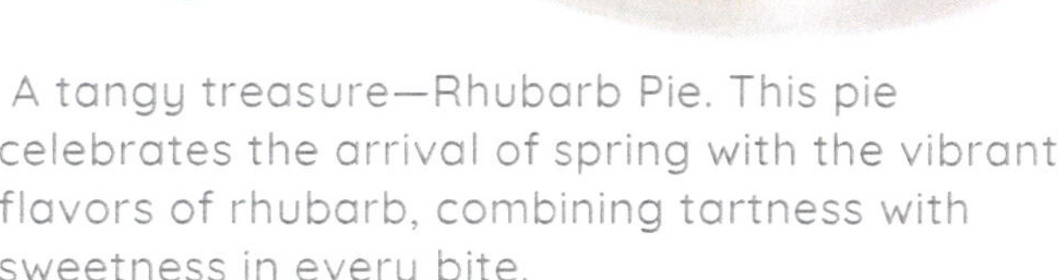

A tangy treasure—Rhubarb Pie. This pie celebrates the arrival of spring with the vibrant flavors of rhubarb, combining tartness with sweetness in every bite.

Ingredients:

For crust: 1 1/4 cups all-purpose flour, 1/2 tsp salt, 1/2 cup unsalted butter (cold, cubed), 3 to 4 tbsp ice water

For filling: 4 cups rhubarb (sliced), 1 1/4 cups granulated sugar, 1/4 cup all-purpose flour, 1/4 tsp ground cinnamon, 1 tbsp butter (cubed)

Substitutions

Lemon zest

Directions

For crust:
1. Mix flour and salt.
2. Cut in cold butter until mixture resembles coarse crumbs.
3. Add ice water, a tablespoon at a time, until dough forms.
4. Shape dough into a disk, chill.
For filling:
1. Preheat oven, roll out dough, fit into pie dish.
2. In a bowl, mix rhubarb, sugar, flour, and cinnamon.
3. Pour mixture into pie crust.
4. Dot with butter cubes.
5. Roll out remaining dough, cover pie, crimp edges.
6. Bake until filling is bubbly and crust is golden.
7. Savor the tangy and sweet medley.

6 servings

380 cal

2 hrs 30 mins

Boiled Dinner with Corned Beef

A hearty tradition—Boiled Dinner with Corned Beef. This dish brings family together, with tender corned beef, potatoes, carrots, and cabbage boiled to perfection, a comforting ode to togetherness.

Ingredients:

3 lbs corned beef brisket, 6 cups water, 2 bay leaves, 10 whole black peppercorns, 6 medium potatoes (peeled and halved), 6 carrots (peeled and halved), 1 head cabbage (cut into wedges), mustard for serving

Substitutions

Horseradish, turnips

Directions

1. In a large pot, place corned beef, water, bay leaves, and peppercorns.
2. Bring to a boil, reduce heat, cover, and simmer for 2 hours.
3. Add potatoes and carrots, simmer for 20 minutes.
4. Add cabbage wedges, simmer for an additional 10 minutes.
5. Remove corned beef and let rest before slicing.
6. Serve vegetables alongside sliced corned beef.
7. Offer mustard for dipping.
8. Savor the hearty flavors of togetherness.

4 servings   240 cal   25 mins

Lobster Salad

A coastal treat—Lobster Salad. This elegant salad showcases succulent lobster meat, paired with fresh greens and a light dressing, a taste of the sea's sophistication.

Ingredients:

2 lobsters (cooked and meat removed), 6 cups mixed salad greens, 1/4 cup red onion (thinly sliced), 1/4 cup cherry tomatoes (halved), 1/4 cup cucumber (sliced), 1/4 cup avocado (diced), 1/4 cup vinaigrette dressing

Directions

1. Prepare lobster meat, ensuring it's free of shell fragments.
2. In a bowl, toss salad greens with red onion, cherry tomatoes, cucumber, and avocado.
3. Arrange lobster meat over the salad.
4. Drizzle vinaigrette dressing over the top.
5. Gently toss to combine flavors.
6. Plate and enjoy the coastal elegance.

Substitutions

Fresh herbs, lemon zest

1 loaf   220 cal   1 hr 15 mins

Pumpkin Bread

A harvest delight—Pumpkin Bread. This moist and flavorful bread captures the essence of autumn, blending the richness of pumpkin with warm spices, a comforting slice of the season.

Ingredients:

1 3/4 cups all-purpose flour, 1 tsp baking soda, 1/2 tsp salt, 1/2 tsp ground cinnamon, 1/2 tsp ground nutmeg, 1/4 tsp ground cloves, 1/4 tsp ground allspice, 1/4 cup unsalted butter (softened), 1 1/2 cups granulated sugar, 2 large eggs, 1 cup pumpkin puree, 1/2 cup water

Substitutions

Walnuts, raisins

Directions

1. Preheat oven and grease a loaf pan.
2. In a bowl, whisk flour, baking soda, salt, and spices.
3. In another bowl, cream butter and sugar until light.
4. Beat in eggs, then pumpkin puree.
5. Gradually add dry ingredients and water, alternating.
6. Pour batter into the prepared pan.
7. Bake until a toothpick comes out clean.
8. Allow to cool before slicing.
9. Savor the warmth of autumn flavors.

4 servings   300 cal   1 hr

Stuffed Acorn Squash

A savory delight—Stuffed Acorn Squash. This dish pairs roasted acorn squash with a flavorful stuffing of grains, vegetables, and herbs, a cozy and wholesome feast that's as pleasing to the eyes as it is to the palate.

Ingredients:

2 acorn squash (halved and seeds removed), 1 cup quinoa, 2 cups vegetable broth, 1/2 cup onion (diced), 1/2 cup celery (diced), 1/2 cup carrots (diced), 1/2 cup bell pepper (diced), 1/2 cup dried cranberries, 1/4 cup pecans (chopped), 2 tbsp olive oil, 1 tsp dried thyme, salt and pepper to taste

Substitutions

Feta cheese

Directions

1. Preheat oven, brush squash halves with olive oil.
2. Roast squash in the oven until tender.
3. Rinse quinoa, cook in vegetable broth.
4. In a pan, sauté onion, celery, carrots, and bell pepper in olive oil.
5. Mix cooked quinoa, sautéed vegetables, cranberries, pecans, thyme, salt, and pepper.
6. Stuff roasted squash halves with the quinoa mixture.
7. Return to the oven briefly to warm the stuffing.
8. Serve and enjoy the nourishing flavors.

10 servings   380 cal   3 hrs

Maple-Glazed Roasted Turkey

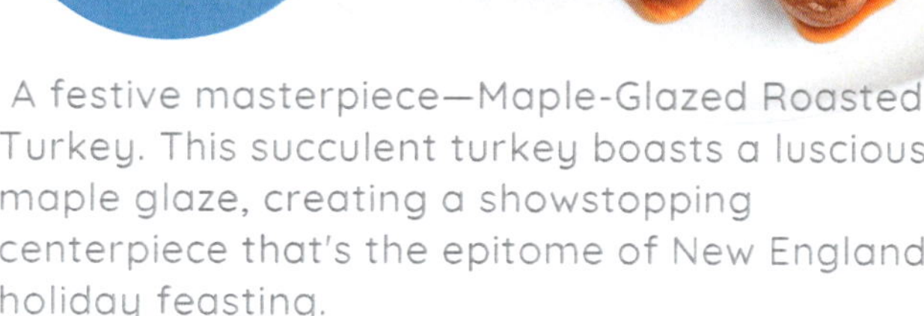

A festive masterpiece—Maple-Glazed Roasted Turkey. This succulent turkey boasts a luscious maple glaze, creating a showstopping centerpiece that's the epitome of New England holiday feasting.

Ingredients:

1 whole turkey (10-12 lbs), 1 cup maple syrup, 1/2 cup unsalted butter (melted), 1/4 cup orange juice, 1 tbsp Dijon mustard, 1 tbsp chopped fresh rosemary, salt and pepper to taste

Substitutions

Thyme sprigs

Directions

1. Preheat oven and prepare turkey.
2. In a bowl, whisk together maple syrup, melted butter, orange juice, Dijon mustard, and chopped rosemary.
3. Season turkey inside and out with salt and pepper.
4. Brush turkey with maple glaze.
5. Roast turkey, brushing with glaze periodically.
6. Cover turkey with foil if it browns too quickly.
7. Turkey is done when internal temperature reaches 165°F (74°C).
8. Rest before carving.
9. Serve the masterpiece with pride.

4 servings

280 cal

40 mins

New England Lobster Boil

A seaside feast—New England Lobster Boil. This communal meal gathers friends and family around a table laden with lobsters, corn, potatoes, and more, a jovial celebration of New England's coastal bounty.

Ingredients:

2 live lobsters (1 1/2 lbs each), 4 ears corn (husked and halved), 8 small red potatoes, 1 lb littleneck clams, 1 lb mussels, 1/2 lb smoked sausage (sliced), 1/4 cup unsalted butter (melted), lemon wedges for serving

Substitutions

Old Bay seasoning

Directions

1. Fill a large pot with water and bring to a boil.
2. Add potatoes, boil for 15 minutes.
3. Add corn, boil for an additional 5 minutes.
4. Add clams, mussels, and sausage, boil for 5 minutes.
5. Add lobsters, cover and steam for 10-15 minutes.
6. Drain water from pot.
7. Serve lobster boil on a newspaper-covered table.
8. Provide melted butter and lemon wedges.
9. Gather, crack, and relish the coastal feast.

6 servings   320 cal   2 hrs

Apple-Cranberry Stuffed Pork Roast

A festive fusion—Apple-Cranberry Stuffed Pork Roast. This succulent pork roast features a flavorful stuffing of apples, cranberries, and herbs, a harmonious blend that captures the essence of the holidays.

Ingredients:

3 lbs boneless pork loin roast, 2 cups cubed bread, 1 cup diced apples, 1/2 cup dried cranberries, 1/4 cup chopped onion, 1/4 cup chopped celery, 1/4 cup chopped walnuts, 1/4 cup chicken broth, 1 tsp dried sage, 1 tsp dried thyme, salt and pepper to taste

Substitutions

Rosemary

Directions

1. Preheat oven and prepare pork roast.
2. In a bowl, combine cubed bread, diced apples, dried cranberries, chopped onion, chopped celery, chopped walnuts, chicken broth, dried sage, dried thyme, salt, and pepper.
3. Cut a slit in the roast to create a pocket.
4. Stuff the pocket with the bread mixture.
5. Tie the roast with kitchen twine to secure the stuffing.
6. Roast the pork until internal temperature reaches 145°F (63°C).
7. Let the roast rest before slicing.
8. Savor the festive fusion of flavors.

4 servings | 220 cal | 1 hr 15 mins

Baked Stuffed Apples

A cozy treat—Baked Stuffed Apples. This dessert combines tender baked apples with a spiced filling of oats and brown sugar, a heartwarming indulgence that radiates comfort and satisfaction.

Ingredients:

4 large baking apples (such as Granny Smith), 1/2 cup rolled oats, 1/4 cup brown sugar, 1/4 cup chopped walnuts, 1/4 cup raisins, 1 tsp ground cinnamon, 1/4 tsp ground nutmeg, 1/4 cup unsalted butter (melted), vanilla ice cream for serving

Directions

1. Preheat oven and prepare apples.
2. In a bowl, mix rolled oats, brown sugar, chopped walnuts, raisins, ground cinnamon, ground nutmeg, and melted butter.
3. Core the apples, creating a well for the filling.
4. Fill each apple with the oat mixture.
5. Place apples in a baking dish.
6. Bake until apples are tender and filling is golden.
7. Serve warm with a scoop of vanilla ice cream.
8. Relish the comforting flavors of home.

Substitutions

Cranberries, whipped cream

Chapter 11:
Holiday Traditions

12-14 servings

350 cal

4 hrs 30 mins

Thanksgiving Turkey with Stuffing

The centerpiece of gratitude—Thanksgiving Turkey with Stuffing. This perfectly roasted turkey, brimming with fragrant stuffing, epitomizes the joy of the season and the unity of family and friends.

Ingredients:

1 whole turkey (12-14 lbs), 1 cup unsalted butter (softened), 2 cups diced onions, 1 cup diced celery, 1 cup diced apples, 2 cups cubed bread, 1/2 cup chopped fresh parsley, 1 tsp dried sage, 1 tsp dried thyme, salt and pepper to taste

Substitutions

Cranberries, walnuts

Directions

1. Preheat oven and prepare turkey.
2. In a pan, sauté onions, celery, and apples in butter until soft.
3. Combine sautéed mixture with cubed bread, parsley, sage, thyme, salt, and pepper.
4. Loosely stuff the turkey's cavity with the stuffing.
5. Roast the turkey, basting occasionally.
6. Turkey is done when internal temperature reaches 165°F (74°C).
7. Let the turkey rest before carving.
8. Share in the abundance of gratitude.

8 servings | 320 cal | 3 hrs 15 mins

New Year's Day Pork and Sauerkraut

Normal

A savory start—New Year's Day Pork and Sauerkraut. This flavorful dish is a cherished tradition, symbolizing good fortune and unity as the new year unfolds, a hearty and heartwarming feast.

Ingredients:

4 lbs pork loin roast, 2 lbs sauerkraut (drained and rinsed), 2 cups diced onions, 1 cup diced apples, 1/2 cup chicken broth, 1/4 cup brown sugar, 1 tsp caraway seeds, salt and pepper to taste

Substitutions

Mustard, beer

Directions

1. Preheat oven and prepare pork roast.
2. Sear pork on all sides in a pan.
3. In a bowl, mix sauerkraut, diced onions, diced apples, chicken broth, brown sugar, and caraway seeds.
4. Place half of the sauerkraut mixture in a roasting pan.
5. Place pork on top of the sauerkraut mixture.
6. Cover the pork with the remaining sauerkraut mixture.
7. Roast until pork is cooked through.
8. Rest before slicing and serving.
9. Begin the year with flavors of togetherness.

10-12 servings   280 cal   3 hrs

Christmas Baked Ham

A holiday classic—Christmas Baked Ham. This succulent ham, adorned with a glaze of brown sugar and spices, embodies the festive spirit of Christmas and beckons loved ones to gather around the table.

Ingredients:

1 bone-in spiral-cut ham (8-10 lbs), 1 cup brown sugar, 1/2 cup Dijon mustard, 1/4 cup pineapple juice, 1/4 cup maple syrup, 1 tsp ground cloves

Substitutions

Pineapple rings

Directions

1. Preheat oven and prepare ham.
2. In a bowl, mix brown sugar, Dijon mustard, pineapple juice, maple syrup, and ground cloves.
3. Place ham in a roasting pan.
4. Brush ham with the glaze mixture.
5. Cover ham with foil.
6. Bake ham, periodically brushing with glaze.
7. Uncover ham for the last 30 minutes of baking.
8. Let ham rest before slicing.
9. Celebrate with a taste of joy.

8 servings

340 cal

2 hrs 30 mins

Easter Leg of Lamb

A springtime tradition—Easter Leg of Lamb. This tender and flavorful roast, adorned with aromatic herbs, embodies the renewal and warmth of Easter, a feast that brings loved ones together in jubilation.

Ingredients:

1 leg of lamb (6-8 lbs), 1/4 cup olive oil, 4 cloves garlic (minced), 2 tbsp chopped fresh rosemary, 1 tbsp chopped fresh thyme, 1 tsp dried oregano, salt and pepper to taste

Directions

1. Preheat oven and prepare leg of lamb.
2. In a bowl, mix olive oil, minced garlic, chopped rosemary, chopped thyme, dried oregano, salt, and pepper.
3. Rub the mixture all over the lamb.
4. Place lamb in a roasting pan.
5. Roast lamb until internal temperature reaches 145°F (63°C).
6. Let lamb rest before slicing.
7. Embrace the joy of Easter feasting.

Substitutions

Lemon zest

6 servings

320 cal

1 hr 45 mins

A patriotic feast—Fourth of July Clambake. This seaside tradition brings friends and family together around a steaming pot of clams, lobster, corn, and more, celebrating the nation's birthday with flavors of the sea.

Fourth of July Clambake

Ingredients:

2 live lobsters (1 1/4 lbs each), 18 littleneck clams, 6 ears corn (husked and halved), 12 small red potatoes, 2 smoked sausages (sliced), 1 lb mussels, 1/4 cup melted butter, lemon wedges for serving

Substitutions

Old Bay seasoning

Directions

1. Fill a large pot with water and bring to a boil.
2. Add potatoes, boil for 15 minutes.
3. Add lobsters and clams, steam for 5 minutes.
4. Add corn, mussels, and sausage, steam for an additional 5 minutes.
5. Drain water from the pot.
6. Serve the clambake on a newspaper-covered table.
7. Provide melted butter and lemon wedges.
8. Celebrate with a feast by the sea.

8 servings

290 cal

1 hr 15 mins

Pumpkin Bread Pudding

Autumnal indulgence—Pumpkin Bread Pudding. This luscious dessert captures the essence of fall with pumpkin, spices, and rich custard-soaked bread, a treat that embraces the comforts of the season.

Ingredients:

8 cups cubed day-old bread, 1 1/2 cups pumpkin puree, 1 cup heavy cream, 1 cup milk, 3/4 cup brown sugar, 4 large eggs, 1 tsp ground cinnamon, 1/2 tsp ground nutmeg, 1/4 tsp ground cloves, 1/4 tsp ground ginger, 1/4 tsp salt, 1 tsp vanilla extract, powdered sugar for dusting

Substitutions

Whipped cream

Directions

1. Preheat oven and prepare a baking dish.
2. Arrange cubed bread in the baking dish.
3. In a bowl, whisk together pumpkin puree, heavy cream, milk, brown sugar, eggs, ground cinnamon, ground nutmeg, ground cloves, ground ginger, salt, and vanilla extract.
4. Pour the mixture over the bread, pressing the bread down to soak.
5. Let the mixture sit for about 30 minutes.
6. Bake until the pudding is set and golden.
7. Dust with powdered sugar before serving.
8. Revel in the taste of autumn's embrace.

8 servings

280 cal

1 hr 30 mins

Cranberry Nut Pie

Tart and sweet delight—Cranberry Nut Pie. This seasonal pie combines the tangy brightness of cranberries with the richness of nuts and custard, a dessert that's as lovely on the holiday table as it is satisfying to the palate.

Ingredients:

1 pie crust (store-bought or homemade), 2 cups fresh cranberries, 1 cup chopped pecans, 3/4 cup granulated sugar, 1/2 cup all-purpose flour, 1/4 cup unsalted butter (melted), 2 large eggs, 1 tsp vanilla extract, whipped cream for serving

Substitutions

Orange zest

Directions

1. Preheat oven and prepare the pie crust.
2. Spread cranberries and chopped pecans in the pie crust.
3. In a bowl, whisk granulated sugar, all-purpose flour, melted butter, eggs, and vanilla extract until smooth.
4. Pour the mixture over the cranberries and pecans.
5. Bake until the filling is set and the top is golden.
6. Let the pie cool before slicing.
7. Serve with a dollop of whipped cream.
8. Enjoy the harmonious dance of flavors.

6-8 servings   350 cal   3 hrs

Irish-American Corned Beef and Cabbage (St. Patrick's Day)

A spirited celebration—Corned Beef and Cabbage for St. Patrick's Day. This beloved dish embraces the Irish-American tradition, offering tender corned beef, hearty vegetables, and a sense of shared heritage.

Ingredients:

4-5 lbs corned beef brisket, 8 small red potatoes, 4 large carrots (peeled and cut into chunks), 1 small head cabbage (cored and cut into wedges), 1 onion (peeled and cut into wedges), 4 cloves garlic (minced), 1 tsp whole black peppercorns, 1 tsp dried thyme, 1 tsp dried parsley, 1 tsp dried mustard, water

Substitutions

Mustard, horseradish

Directions

1. Rinse the corned beef under cold water.
2. Place corned beef in a large pot and cover with water.
3. Add black peppercorns, dried thyme, dried parsley, dried mustard, and minced garlic.
4. Bring to a boil, then reduce heat to a simmer and cover.
5. Simmer for about 2 hours, skimming off any foam.
6. Add whole vegetables and continue simmering for another hour.
7. Remove corned beef and let it rest before slicing.
8. Serve with the tender vegetables.
9. Enjoy the Irish-American spirit.

8 servings

320 cal

1 hr 30 mins

Independence Day Blueberry Pie

Berry-filled jubilation—Independence Day Blueberry Pie. This patriotic dessert captures the essence of summer with a medley of fresh blueberries, encased in a flaky crust that radiates the red, white, and blue.

Ingredients:

1 pie crust (store-bought or homemade), 5 cups fresh blueberries, 3/4 cup granulated sugar, 1/4 cup cornstarch, 1/2 tsp ground cinnamon, 1 tbsp lemon juice, 1 tbsp unsalted butter (cut into small pieces), egg wash (1 egg beaten with 1 tbsp water)

Substitutions

Vanilla ice cream

Directions

1. Preheat oven and prepare the pie crust.
2. In a bowl, mix blueberries, granulated sugar, cornstarch, ground cinnamon, and lemon juice.
3. Pour the blueberry mixture into the pie crust.
4. Dot the filling with butter pieces.
5. Roll out the second pie crust and cut into strips for a lattice top.
6. Create a lattice pattern on top of the pie.
7. Trim and crimp the edges.
8. Brush the lattice with egg wash.
9. Bake until the filling is bubbly and the crust is golden.
10. Celebrate with a slice of Americana.

8 servings   340 cal   1 hr 45 mins

New England Maple Cream Pie

Syrupy sweetness—New England Maple Cream Pie. This divine dessert marries the rich flavors of maple syrup and cream in a tender crust, capturing the essence of New England's cherished maple traditions.

Ingredients:

1 pie crust (store-bought or homemade), 3/4 cup pure maple syrup, 1 1/2 cups heavy cream, 1/4 cup granulated sugar, 1/4 cup cornstarch, 4 large egg yolks, 1/4 tsp salt, 1 tsp vanilla extract, whipped cream for serving

Substitutions

None

Directions

1. Preheat oven and prepare the pie crust.
2. In a saucepan, heat maple syrup and 1 cup of heavy cream.
3. In a bowl, whisk granulated sugar, cornstarch, egg yolks, and salt.
4. Gradually add the hot cream mixture to the egg mixture, whisking constantly.
5. Return the mixture to the saucepan and cook until thickened.
6. Remove from heat and stir in vanilla extract.
7. Pour the custard into the pie crust.
8. Bake until the custard is set.
9. Let the pie cool before slicing.
10. Serve with a dollop of whipped cream.
11. Relish the harmonious flavors of maple.

We need your help

As we reach the end of this culinary journey we'd like to ask for your support. Reviews are indeed hard to come by, and if you've enjoyed this book and found our recipes delightful, we kindly request that you take a moment to share your thoughts.

Please go back to your app or the platform where you made your purchase, click on the review button, and give us a rating along with a short sentence about your experience. Your feedback means the world to us.

Being a small publisher, reviews are a precious resource that can make a significant difference for us. Your review could help us drastically in reaching more readers who share your passion for New England comfort cuisine.

Rest assured, we read and appreciate every single review, and your input is invaluable to us. If you happen to come across any small mistakes, please understand that we've done our best to provide you with an exceptional cookbook. However, as in any creative endeavor, sometimes mistakes can slip through. We hope you can overlook them and focus on the love and dedication that went into every recipe.